Know, Love & Live the Catholic Faith
249 Pollard, John E, Rev.
Pol

Know, Love, and Live the Catholic Faith

Reverend John E. Pollard

Our Sunday Visitor Publishing Division
Our Sunday Visitor, Inc.
Huntington, Indiana 46750

Nihil Obstat: Rev. Michael Heintz
Censor Librorum

Imprimatur: ✠ John M. D'Arcy
Bishop of Fort Wayne-South Bend
July 28, 2005

The *Nihil Obstat* and *Imprimatur* are official declarations that a book or pamphlet is free from doctrinal or moral error. It is not implied that those who have granted the *Nihil Obstat* and *Imprimatur* agree with the contents, opinions, or statements expressed.

For my father and mother,
Michael and Lauretta Pollard,
my lifelong catechists.

Table of Contents

Introduction

In the years following the Second Vatican Council, no other aspect of the Church's pastoral mission has been the subject of as many significant documents as has catechesis. The council's *Decree on the Pastoral Office of Bishops in the Church* called for the renewal of catechesis in general and "a directory for the catechetical instruction of the Christian people" (n. 41) in particular.

As a result, in 1971 the Holy See promulgated the *General Catechetical Directory*, which urged episcopal conferences around the world to develop national catechetical directories. In 1979 the bishops of the United States published *Sharing the Light of Faith: The National Catechetical Directory for Catholics in the United States*. As a young seminarian I participated in the consultations that preceded this national directory. The Extraordinary Synod of Bishops of 1985 expressed the "desire that a catechism or compendium of all Catholic doctrine regarding both faith and morals be composed" (*Apostolic Constitution on the Publication of the Catechism of the Catholic Church*, Introduction). In 1992 Pope John Paul II promulgated the *Catechism of the Catholic Church*, the first universal compendium of Catholic doctrine to be published in over 500 years. I was privileged to be the American bishops' staff person for the *Catechism* and helped in its preparation and dissemination in this country.

The publication of the *Catechism* was a seismic event in the history of catechesis and occasioned the development of a new *General Directory for Catechesis*. As a member of the International Catechetical Council, I helped draft the outline for the new *General Directory*, which was published in 1997. The new *General Directory*, like its predecessor, urged episcopal conferences around the world to develop new national directories for catechesis. Therefore, in 2005, the bishops of the United States issued the *National Directory for Catechesis*. It was my distinct honor to serve as the special consultant to the committee of bishops that prepared the new *National Directory.*

This extraordinary series of events points to a new moment in catechesis, a new opportunity for the renewal of catechesis called for by the Second Vatican Council. This new moment is especially important for those seeking to become Catholic or those Catholics interested in deepening their knowledge and love of the Catholic faith. Along with this opportunity comes the responsibility to provide them with an experience of evangelization and catechesis that is sensitive and sensible, formational and informational. I hope *Know, Love, and Live the Catholic Faith* does precisely that.

In my experience as a parish priest, the numbers of those who seek baptism, those who seek full communion with the Catholic Church, those who wish to renew and deepen their faith, and those who would like to return to the practice of their faith have steadily been increasing. The most dramatic rise in numbers has come from those who drifted away from the Church and who now seek to "come home" again. Some have been alienated from the Church, and some have merely been lax. They most often come forward at key moments of their lives — the sacramental moments — with a genuine faith that has remained alive, if somewhat dormant. These people may not be able to articulate precisely why they seek marriage in the Church or why they want to have their children baptized and raised as Catholics or why they think it is time they were confirmed in the Catholic faith, but they are clearly reaching out and they deserve a warm welcome.

In writing this book, it was my intention to provide a clear and manageable summary of Catholic faith, Catholic life, and Catholic practice within the context of scriptural reflection, questions for group discussion, questions for personal reflection, and prayer. I sincerely hope that this text will serve the reader's general interest or particular need to know about the Catholic faith, to talk with others about the Catholic faith, to pray with others, to reflect more personally, and to feel welcomed as a vital member of the Church.

Each chapter begins with a scriptural text on the particular theme of the chapter; this is followed by a short introduction to the material that will be covered in the chapter. Following next are study questions; these are questions that my parishioners have actually asked over the years. The responses to these questions are my attempts to reply as honestly and briefly as I can. Next come questions for group discussion that lend themselves to comfortable dialogue and that flow directly from the study questions. Questions for personal reflection, which are intended to be of a more private, thoughtful nature, are also provided so that the reader has an opportunity to integrate the experience into his or her own life. Finally, a prayer is included that can serve either as a closing prayer for a group session or as the reader's personal prayer.

There are three major parts to *Know, Love, and Live the Catholic Faith* that can be used in either a group or an individual catechetical setting: "Catholic Faith" focuses on the living Tradition of the Church; "Catholic Life" treats the person's lived response of faith; "Catholic Practice" outlines the basic actions performed by Catholics.

Faith is the free gift of God. No catechist can provide it. An intelligent and sensitive experience of coming to know the Catholic faith — how it is lived and how it is shared in the community of faith — can encourage all those interested to accept the gift of faith and stimulate their growth in faith. *Know, Love, and Live the Catholic Faith* is a means toward that end, for the catechetical process is a relationship of persons, to one another and to the Lord.

FATHER JOHN POLLARD

PART ONE

Catholic Faith

In the Catholic tradition, faith is the fusion of believing, trusting, and doing. Part of our faith involves learning and knowing the basic teachings of the Catholic Church. Part of our faith involves trusting the reliability of an eternal God who saves us through Jesus' love. And part of our faith involves the personal commitment of genuine Christian living. It is a dynamic, integrating process that absorbs the whole person.

First of all, faith entails discovering what the Church authoritatively teaches, probing that discovery, and giving the firm assent of mind. In other words, part of our faith is our affirmation of the basic teachings held by Catholics. In order to give that affirmation to the tenets of the Catholic faith, we need to know the core content of what the Church holds and teaches.

The first section of this exploration of the Catholic faith guides you through the basic teachings of the Catholic Church. It is important to note that these basic teachings are the Church's responses to the fundamental questions men and women have been asking since the beginning of time. They are not abstract assertions, unrelated to real people in real life situations.

The topics covered in this first section include:

- **Revelation** — offers a response to our natural need to know what God has communicated to us in the past and how he shows himself to us in the present.
- **Faith** — responds to our questions about the difference faith makes in our lives here on earth and in eternity.
- **God** — probes the questions most people have about God's existence, how we come to know God, and the possibilities of our relationship with God.
- **Jesus Christ** — treats the issue of how Jesus can be God and man at the same time, how he could have been born of a virgin, and what his death and resurrection mean for us.
- **The Holy Spirit** — establishes in the Trinity a relationship between the Father and Jesus, a bond of love, and the principle of life and enthusiasm in the Church today.
- **Sacred Scripture** — deals with God's inspiration of the writers of the Bible, how the books of the Bible were collected, the truths they contain, and some suggestions for proper use of Sacred Scripture.
- **The Church** — discusses Church membership, authority in the Church, and the Church's essential purpose.
- **Mary** — explains how our Blessed Lady was really Jesus' mother and yet remained a virgin, how she was preserved from sin from the first moment of her life, and how she was assumed into heaven at the end of her earthly life.
- **The Future** — deals with our curiosity about the immortality of the soul, the afterlife, the final judgment, and the Kingdom of God.
- **Grace** — addresses our questions about the effects of God's love in our lives, the nature of freedom, and predestination.
- **Man** — explores our questions about the creation of man and woman, their destiny, original sin, free will, and the soul.

CHAPTER 1
Revelation

———

SCRIPTURE REFLECTION

Leading the flock across the desert, [Moses] came to Horeb, the mountain of God. There an angel of the LORD appeared to him in fire flaming out of a bush. As he looked on, he was surprised to see that the bush, though on fire, was not consumed. So Moses decided, "I must go over to look at this remarkable sight, and see why the bush is not burned."

When the LORD saw him coming over to look at it more closely, God called out to him from the bush, "Moses! Moses!" He answered, "Here I am." God said, "Come no nearer! Remove the sandals from your feet, for the place where you stand is holy ground. I am the God of your father," he continued, "the God of Abraham, the God of Isaac, the God of Jacob." Moses hid his face, for he was afraid to look at God....

"But," said Moses to God, "when I go to the Israelites and say to them, 'The God of your fathers has sent me to you,' if they ask me, 'What is his name?' what am I to tell them?" God replied, "I am who am." Then he added, "This is what you shall tell the Israelites: I AM sent me to you."

EXODUS 3:1-6, 13-14

INTRODUCTION

"God so loved the world that he gave his only Son" (Jn 3:16). The story of God's relationship to all of creation is a story of love. Throughout the history of the human race, God has continually offered love freely, a love that he initiated, a love that we did not merit. In the beginning God demonstrated his love through the wonders of creation, especially in the creation of man and woman. The Scriptures reveal over and over again the renewal of God's loving promise to be with his people. This commitment reaches its fulfillment in the life, death, and resurrection of Jesus.

Our journey in faith is, for the most part, an adventure that seeks to discover who God is, who we are, and what kind of relationship exists between God and ourselves. We do not make this journey alone, but rather we join with others who ask many of the same questions and who seek reasonable responses to them. This adventure has been a common theme running through the ages, the concern of men and women of every race and nation. This is salvation history, a history whose beginning, middle, and end are concerned with God's constant, loving invitation to love him in return. We are related to God in a covenant, which is a commitment and a pact of faithful love.

STUDY QUESTIONS

1. What is Revelation?

Revelation is God's gift of himself to humanity. It is his utterly free communication of himself through which he makes known the mystery of his divine plan. God realizes this plan through his words and actions that make up the history of salvation. "God has fully revealed this plan by sending us his beloved Son, our Lord Jesus Christ, and the Holy Spirit" (CCC 50).

2. Why is Revelation important?

God's revelation of himself and his plan of loving goodness is central to Christian life. By revealing himself to us, God communicates his own divine life to us and demonstrates his eternal will that all people should share his divine nature and live in communion with him. Through his revelation, God enables us to respond to him, to know him, and to love him. In his revelation, God has "provided the definitive, super-abundant answer to the questions that man asks himself about the meaning and purpose of his life" (CCC 68).

3. How does God reveal himself?

God reveals himself gradually and in stages, naturally and super-naturally. In the beginning God made himself known in creation, especially in the creation of human life, and he continues to provide evidence of himself in the created order.

4. How does God reveal himself naturally in creation?

While God had no need to create, he chose to share the blessing of existence itself. God is the source of all that exists, and his creation is "very good" (Gn 1:31). God created the human person in his own image. Thus, in the goodness, beauty, and wonder of creation, God revealed himself. "In the creation of the world and of man, God gave the first and universal witness to his almighty love and his wisdom, the first proclamation of his 'plan of loving goodness,' which finds its goal in the new creation in Christ" (CCC 315).

5. How does God reveal himself supernaturally?

Because he desires all people to be saved, God chose to insert himself in the history of the Israelite people by pledging his faithful and enduring love. God first established the covenant as a sign of his love with our first parents and renewed it with Noah, Abraham, and Moses. In Jesus Christ, God brings his revelation to completion because Jesus is the fulfillment of God's faithful and enduring love. "God has revealed himself fully by sending his own Son, in whom he has established his covenant for ever. The Son is the Father's definitive Word; so there will be no further Revelation after him" (CCC 73).

6. How is Jesus the fullness of God's revelation?

Everything that God has to communicate to us is fulfilled in the life, death, and resurrection of Jesus, as well as in the sending of the

Holy Spirit. God's love is completely revealed in the person of Jesus. He is at once *what* God has to say to us and *how* he speaks to us — that is to say, Jesus is both the means God uses to reach us and the content of the message he has for us. "Christ, the Son of God made man, is the Father's one, perfect, and unsurpassable Word. In him he has said everything; there will be no other word than this one" (CCC 65).

7. *How does God reveal himself in Sacred Scripture?*
Sacred Scripture, or the Bible, is the record of divine Revelation. God himself is the author of Sacred Scripture. He acts in and through the human authors of the Bible to communicate his saving truth without error. The Bible is a collection of books comprised of the Old Testament and the New Testament. The four Gospels of the New Testament hold a pivotal place within Sacred Scripture because Jesus Christ is their center. "*Sacred Scripture* is the speech of God as it is put down in writing under the breath of the Holy Spirit" (*DV* 9) (CCC 81). In summary, Sacred Scripture contains the Word of God written down under the inspiration of the Holy Spirit.

8. *What does "inspiration" mean?*
Inspiration is the gift of the Holy Spirit given by God to the authors of the books of Sacred Scripture so that they could express the saving truth of God's Word. "God inspired the human authors of the sacred books. 'To compose the sacred books, God chose certain men who, all the while he employed them in this task, made full use of their own faculties and powers so that, though he acted in them and by them, it was as true authors that they consigned to writing whatever he wanted written, and no more' (*DV* 11)" (CCC 106). Inspiration, then, is not the mysterious alteration of human writings by God's action; neither does inspiration remove Sacred Scripture from the cultural context in which it was produced. It is God's own word communicated faithfully through human authors.

9. Is Sacred Scripture free from error?

Because it is the inspired Word of God, Sacred Scripture reveals without error the truth God intended to be revealed by it. Sacred Scripture is a uniquely reliable witness to God's revelation and does not falsify what God intended to communicate. "God is the author of Sacred Scripture because he inspired its human authors; he acts in them and by means of them. He thus gives assurance that their writings teach without error his saving truth (cf. *DV* 11)" (CCC 136).

Sacred Scripture was not, however, miraculously preserved from historical or scientific errors; the writers, even though they were inspired, were nevertheless subject to the limitations of human knowledge and language and the culture of their age. Sacred Scripture is to be interpreted both literally and spiritually.

10. How are we to interpret Sacred Scripture correctly?

In order to interpret Sacred Scripture correctly, we should seek to discover what God intends to reveal to us for our salvation through the inspired writers. We should, first of all, interpret Sacred Scripture in the light of the same Holy Spirit who inspired it. We should take into account the conditions of the writers' times and cultures as well as their languages and literary forms.

There are three criteria for the interpretation of Sacred Scripture. "1. *Be especially attentive 'to the content and unity of the whole of Scripture.'* ... 2. *Read the Scripture within the 'living Tradition of the whole Church.'* ... 3. *Be attentive to the analogy of faith* (cf. Rom 12:6). By 'analogy of faith' we mean the coherence of the truths of faith among themselves and within the whole plan of Revelation" (CCC 112-114).

Ultimately, the authority for the correct interpretation of Sacred Scripture rests with the Church because she has been entrusted by God with the ministry of guarding and interpreting the Word of God.

11. What is Tradition?

Christ commissioned his apostles to preach the Gospel to all nations until the end of time. The apostles, in turn, entrusted this commission to their successors. The living transmission of the Gospel in the Church is Tradition. The teaching of the apostles and their successors (Tradition) and the written Word of God (Sacred Scripture) together make up a single sacred deposit of the Word of God. God's revelation is the common origin of both Tradition and Sacred Scripture. "Through Tradition, 'the Church, in her doctrine, life, and worship perpetuates and transmits to every generation all that she herself is, all that she believes' (*DV* 8 § 1)" (CCC 78).

12. How are we to interpret Tradition correctly?

The apostles entrusted the deposit of the faith, contained in Sacred Scripture and Tradition, to the whole Church. The authority to interpret the Word of God rests with the teaching office of the Church (Magisterium). The teaching office of the Church is comprised of the bishops in communion with the Pope as the head of the college of bishops. It is the servant of the Word of God and teaches only what has been handed on to it. The teaching office of the Church only proposes for belief as being divinely revealed that which is found in the single deposit of faith. "The Church's Magisterium exercises the authority it holds from Christ to the fullest extent when it defines dogmas, that is, when it proposes, in a form obliging the Christian people to an irrevocable adherence of faith, truths contained in divine Revelation or also when it proposes, in a definitive way, truths having a necessary connection with these" (CCC 88).

13. What is the deposit of faith?

The deposit of faith is the heritage of faith contained in Sacred Scripture and Tradition that has been entrusted to the whole Church. It has been handed on from one generation of the faithful to another since the time of the apostles." 'By adhering to [this heritage] the entire holy people, united to its pastors, remains always faithful to the teaching of the apostles, to the brotherhood, to the breaking of bread and the prayers. So, in maintaining, practicing, and professing the faith that has been handed on, there should be a remarkable harmony between the bishops and the faithful' (*DV* 10 § 1; cf. Acts 2:42 [Gk.]; Pius XII, apostolic constitution, *Munificentissimus Deus*, November 1, 1950: AAS 42 [1950], 756, taken along with the words of St. Cyprian, *Epist.* 66, 8: CSEL 3, 2, 733: 'The Church is the people united to its Priests, the flock adhering to its Shepherd')" (CCC 84).

14. **What is the relationship between Sacred Scripture and Tradition?**
Although Sacred Scripture and Tradition originate in one common source, God's revelation, they form two distinct modes for the transmission of that revelation. Sacred Scripture communicates the message of salvation under the inspiration of the Holy Spirit. "*Tradition* transmits in its entirety the Word of God which has been entrusted to the apostles by Christ the Lord and the Holy Spirit. It transmits it to the successors of the apostles so that, enlightened by the Spirit of truth, they may faithfully preserve, expound, and spread it abroad by their preaching' (*DV* 9)" (CCC 81). Sacred Scripture and Tradition flow from the same well-spring and are bound closely together. "Each of them makes present and fruitful in the Church the mystery of Christ" (CCC 80).

QUESTIONS FOR GROUP DISCUSSION

1. What is God's covenant?
2. Who are God's people?
3. Can the covenant relationship be ruptured or severed?
4. Where did Sacred Scripture come from?

5. How can I understand Sacred Scripture?

6. How can I use Sacred Scripture in my daily life?

QUESTIONS FOR PERSONAL REFLECTION

1. Why does God love me?

2. Why does God choose to reveal himself to me?

3. What do I seek in my relationship with God?

4. How do I respond to God's love for me?

5. Am I alone in a relationship with God?

6. How do I feel that God continues to reveal himself to me?

PRAYER BEFORE READING SACRED SCRIPTURE

Lord, open my mind that I may receive your holy word and live according to your plan. Open my eyes that I may see the marvelous truths in your laws. Instruct me in your statutes that with my lips I will declare your praise. Bless me so I can fully treasure your word as I seek you with all my heart. Send your Holy Spirit to guide me along the path you have set for me. Amen.

CHAPTER 2

Faith

———

SCRIPTURE REFLECTION

For by grace you have been saved through faith, and this is not from you; it is the gift of God; it is not from works, so no one may boast.

EPHESIANS 2:8-9

INTRODUCTION

Since faith is a personal, trusting response to God's communication of himself, it is ultimately a mysterious experience that cannot be understood in the same way that we can understand scientific facts. Basically, faith is a gift that is freely given by God. Because of our freedom, we can choose to reject God's invitation to faith, but we should not confuse such rejection with mere doubt. The *Catechism of the Catholic Church* teaches:

> Faith is a personal act — the free response of the human person to the initiative of God who reveals himself. But faith is not an isolated act. No one can believe alone, just as no one can live alone. You have not given yourself faith as you have not given yourself life. The believer has received faith from others and should hand it on to others. Our love for Jesus and for our neighbor impels us to speak to others about our faith. Each believer is thus a link in the great chain of believers. I cannot believe without being carried by the faith of others, and by my faith I help support others in the faith [CCC 166].

The Christian life is a life of searching, of discovery, of adventure, and it naturally seeks deeper insights into the meaning of life itself. Such a journey may sometimes reveal doubts, even about God himself, but these doubts do not necessarily indicate a lack of faith or a weak faith. In fact, they may demonstrate a developing faith that is vibrant and genuinely seeking the resolution of the original doubts. Our journey in faith is a lifelong process that seeks to understand the very mystery of God himself. Throughout our lives we will need to read, to discuss with others, to think, and to pray over the gift of our faith, for what makes sense to us as children ordinarily will not be sufficient to satisfy our more mature questions.

STUDY QUESTIONS

1. What is faith?

"Faith is first of all a personal adherence of man to God. At the same time, and inseparably, it is a *free assent to the whole truth that God has revealed*" (CCC 150). Faith is both divine initiative and human response. It is a gift of God and a personal act. Faith is a theological virtue infused by God into the souls of the faithful "by which we believe in God and believe all that he has said and revealed to us, and that Holy Church proposes for our belief, because he is truth itself" (CCC 1814). Faith is professed in the Creed, celebrated in the sacraments, lived out in the moral life, and expressed in prayer.

2. Where does faith come from?

Faith is a gift from God that is freely given and freely accepted. "When St. Peter confessed that Jesus is the Christ, the Son of the living God, Jesus declared to him that this revelation did not come 'from flesh and blood,' but from 'my Father who is in heaven' (Mt 16:17; cf. Gal 1:15; Mt 11:25)" (CCC 153).

3. What is the obedience of faith?

The obedience of faith is the believer's free assent to the Word of God because it has been revealed by God and its truth is guaranteed by God, who is Truth itself. "*By faith*, man completely submits his intellect and his will to God (cf. *DV* 5). With his whole being man gives his assent to God the revealer. Sacred Scripture calls this human response to God, the author of revelation, 'the obedience of faith' (cf. Rom 1:5; 16:26)" (CCC 143). The obedience of faith is by no means contrary to human freedom or human reason. Trusting in God, believing the whole truth he has revealed, and submitting our intellect and will to him is the authentically human response to the gift of God's grace.

4. What difference does faith make?

Faith binds the person to the truth that God has revealed. Faith seeks a deeper understanding of the One who has revealed the truth as well as the truth he has revealed. Faith is decisive in human life because without it salvation is impossible. In other words, faith allows the believer to see the world controlled by the power of good, which penetrates and goes beyond all things. This power is God, and faith in God enables the believer to see meaning rather than random chaos in life. Faith convinces the believer that life is worth living and directing toward good. Faith puts everything in a new light, discloses God's design for human life, and leads us to become fully human.

5. Is faith necessary for salvation?

"Faith is necessary for salvation. The Lord himself affirms: 'He who believes and is baptized will be saved; but he who does not believe will be condemned' (Mk 16:16)" (CCC 183). Unless a person freely responds to God's revelation with faith, that person is not saved. Without a free response of faith, there is no connection between God and the person. "Believing in Jesus Christ and in the One who

sent him for our salvation is necessary for obtaining that salvation"
(cf. Mk 16:16; Jn 3:36; 6:40 et al.) (CCC 161).

6. *Can only Christians be saved?*

God's loving plan of goodness is universal. His will for salvation
extends to all people. All salvation, however, comes from Christ
and through his Body, the Church. Those who knowingly refuse to
recognize Christ or his Church cannot be saved. The Second
Vatican Council teaches, "Those who, through no fault of their
own, do not know the Gospel of Christ or his Church, but who
nevertheless seek God with a sincere heart, and, moved by grace,
try in their actions to do his will as they know it through the dic-
tates of their conscience — those too may achieve eternal salvation" (*Dogmatic Constitution on the Church*, 16).

7. *Is faith sufficient for salvation?*

People who respond to God's revelation with faith cannot sit back
and assume they are saved. If faith is genuine, it is demonstrated
through a life committed to and animated by Christian values,
such as justice, mercy, compassion, and peace. "To live, grow, and
persevere in faith until the end we must nourish it with the word
of God; we must beg the Lord to increase our faith (cf. Mk 9:24; Lk
17:5; 22:32); it must be 'working through charity,' abounding in
hope, and rooted in the faith of the Church (Gal 5:6; Rom 15:13; cf.
Jas 2:14-26)" (CCC 162).

8. *Can I be sure that I am saved?*

All are in need of salvation. Salvation comes from God alone. He
desires the salvation of all. In his loving plan of goodness, the
Father sent his only Son precisely for our salvation. The Church is
the universal instrument and sacrament of salvation. Under the
action of the Holy Spirit, Sacred Scripture, Tradition, the sacraments, and the teaching office of the Church contribute to the salvation of souls. God's gift of faith is certain, but our personal

adherence to the whole truth God has revealed is not. Faith must be expressed in works of charity in order to be authentic. It must be preserved, nourished, professed, witnessed, and spread. We must always hope and pray for personal salvation, for help in attaining it, and for the forgiveness of our sins. But absolute assurance of personal salvation is not possible.

QUESTIONS FOR GROUP DISCUSSION

1. How do I know that I have faith?
2. In what sense is faith a commitment?
3. How does a person come to have faith?
4. Does faith sometimes involve pain?
5. Is faith an internal or external process?
6. Is it wrong to doubt?
7. How can a person lose his or her faith?

QUESTIONS FOR PERSONAL REFLECTION

1. Where did my faith come from?
2. Am I concerned with developing an adult faith?
3. Can I handle uncertainty and doubt?
4. How important are others on my journey in faith?

ACT OF FAITH

O my God, I believe that you are one God in three divine persons: Father, Son, and Holy Spirit. I believe that your divine Son became man and died for our sins, and that he will come to judge the living and the dead. I believe these and all the truths the Catholic Church teaches, because you have revealed them, who can neither deceive nor be deceived. Amen.

CHAPTER 3
God

———

SCRIPTURE REFLECTION

In the year king Uzziah died, I saw the Lord seated on a high and lofty throne, with the train of his garment filling the temple. Seraphim were stationed above; each of them had six wings: with two they veiled their faces, with two they veiled their feet, and with two they hovered aloft.

"Holy, holy, holy is the LORD of hosts!" they cried one to the other. "All the earth is filled with his glory!" At the sound of that cry, the frame of the door shook and the house was filled with smoke.

Then I said, "Woe is me, I am doomed! For I am a man of unclean lips, living among a people of unclean lips, yet my eyes have seen the King, the LORD of Hosts!" Then one of the seraphim flew to me, holding an ember which he had taken with tongs from the altar.

He touched my mouth with it. "See," he said, "now that this has touched your lips, your wickedness is removed, your sin purged."

ISAIAH 6:1-7

INTRODUCTION

From the very beginning of time, humans have understood themselves to be related to a higher power. In different ages and cultures this higher power has taken many forms, but the essential experience of people has been that there is some being beyond themselves, a being who is in some way responsible for their existence. The great gift of the Israelites to the history of belief in supreme power is a belief in a single supreme power who is the ground or reason for the existence of everyone and everything. This mystery, which we call God, has revealed himself to us as Father, Son, and Spirit. This Holy Trinity, then, is three persons — Father, Son, and Spirit — in the unity of one God.

God's activity, the divine economy, is the common work of the three divine persons. The Trinity has only one nature and one operation. However, each divine person performs the common work of the Trinity proper to himself, in accord with his particular attribute. For example, we refer to the Father as Creator of all that is, to the Son as Savior or Redeemer, and to the Spirit as Sanctifier.

> Being a work at once common and personal, the whole divine economy makes known both what is proper to the divine persons and their one divine nature. Hence the whole Christian life is a communion with each of the divine persons, without in any way separating them. Everyone who glorifies the Father does so through the Son in the Holy Spirit; everyone who follows Christ does so because the Father draws him and the Spirit moves him (cf. Jn 6:44; Rom 8:14) [CCC 259].

The Trinity is the fundamental doctrine of the faith. The *Catechism of the Catholic Church* teaches, "The mystery of the Most Holy Trinity is the central mystery of Christian faith and life. It is the mystery of God in himself. It is therefore the source of all the other mysteries of faith, the light that enlightens them" (CCC 234).

STUDY QUESTIONS

1. *Who is God?*
   Any words used to answer this question will reveal the limitations of human language, not any inherent limitations in God. The word

"God" has been used to refer to the "ground of all being," the "ultimate reality." For the Christian, God is the Creator of all that is and the Author of divine Revelation, the Savior of the world, and the Principle of life and unity in the Church — one God in three divine persons. "The God of our faith has revealed himself as He who is; and he has made himself known as 'abounding in steadfast love and faithfulness' (Ex 34:6). God's very being is Truth and Love" (CCC 231).

2. What is the Holy Trinity?

The Holy Trinity is the central mystery of the Christian faith. It cannot be known by human reason alone. "God alone can make it known to us by revealing himself as Father, Son, and Holy Spirit" (CCC 261). By his becoming man, Jesus, the eternal Son, revealed God as his eternal Father with whom he shares the same substance. In the Father and with the Father, the Son is one and the same God. The Holy Spirit proceeds from the communion of both the Father and the Son and, therefore, is co-eternal, is of the same substance, and is the same God as the Father and the Son.

The doctrine of the Holy Trinity is the formulation of the Christian experience of God as three divine persons: Father, Son, and Holy Spirit in one divine nature. The three persons are distinct in their relations — namely, in the sense that the Father is not the Son, the Son is not the Father, and neither the Father nor the Son is the Spirit. But they are one in the sense that there is but one God, the community of the Trinity: Father, Son, and Holy Spirit. "Inseparable in what they are, the divine persons are also inseparable in what they do. But within the single divine operation each shows forth what is proper to him in the Trinity, especially in the divine missions of the Son's Incarnation and the gift of the Holy Spirit" (CCC 267).

3. Can I prove God's existence?

The existence of God cannot be proven in the same sense of proof in the natural sciences — namely, through empirical evidence alone. The certainty of the truth of God's existence is a reasonable conclusion drawn from converging and convincing arguments. One can come to conclude that God exists through creation. The existence of the world, its order and beauty, convinces one that God is the origin and end of the universe. The existence of man and woman — together with their natural desire for God, inherent freedom, innate sense of moral goodness, and longing for happiness and eternity — leads one to conclude that human life has a spiritual dimension, a soul, which could only be placed there by God. Belief in God depends as much on a mind and heart open enough to perceive evidence of God as it does on the gift of faith in which God reveals himself.

Belief in God, therefore, is a result of both faith and reason. The Church has consistently taught that the one true God can be known with certainty from his works by the natural light of human reason. "When he listens to the message of creation and to the voice of conscience, man can arrive at certainty about the existence of God, the cause and end of everything"(CCC 46).

4. *How can I come to know God?*

We can come to a knowledge of the existence of a personal God through faith and reason. "The world, and man, attest that they contain within themselves neither their first principle nor their final end, but rather that they participate in Being itself, which alone is without origin or end. Thus, in different ways, man can come to know that there exists a reality which is the first cause and final end of all things, a reality 'that everyone calls "God" ' (St. Thomas Aquinas, *STh* I, 2, 3)" (CCC 34).

In order to invite us into a real intimacy with him, however, God both revealed himself to us and gave us the grace to welcome that revelation and so come to a deeper knowledge of him. Initially, we come to know God in the world of nature as the reason for order and meaning in life. We come to know him in the history of his covenant relationship with the people of Israel in the Old Testament. Primarily, we come to know God as he discloses himself in Jesus Christ, the manifestation of God's covenant in the New Testament. We come to know God, in whose image we are made, as we probe the meaning of our own existence since he is the source of our life and the object of our love. We also come to know God through the community of the Church.

5. How is God active today?

God is not active in the world in the same sense that a giant corporation is active. God is the reason for the activity of all creation. He gives his creatures being and existence, upholds them and sustains them in being, enables them to act, and brings them to their final end. This plan for creation is called "divine providence." While God is the master of his plan, he "grants his creatures not only their existence, but also the dignity of acting on their own, of being causes and principles for each other, and thus of cooperating in the accomplishment of his plan" (CCC 306).

6. What is meant by "divine providence"?

Divine providence is comprised of "the dispositions by which God guides his creation toward … perfection" (CCC 302). It is his foresight, his abiding love for all creation. It refers to God's active direction of human history toward the goal that he intends for it. It also refers to God's personal intervention in human history. God is the inner principle of life that moves every person, indeed the whole of history, toward its resolution in Christ. God's enduring love for us directs the course of human history without depriving us of our freedom.

7. Does God know all things?

In God there is no limitation whatsoever — no limit of time, place, power, knowledge, love, mercy, or truth. Therefore God is all-knowing. He knows himself immediately and absolutely. He cannot grow in knowledge since he is his own knowledge of himself. He knows all things universally and particularly. He has timeless knowledge of everything that ever exists in time. All things are present to him at once. God is not extremely intelligent in a human sense. Rather God's knowledge extends to all that is, all that ever was and will ever be. "God, who alone made heaven and earth, can alone impart true knowledge of every created thing in relation to himself" (cf. Ps 115:15; Wis 7:17-21) (CCC 216).

8. *If God knows all things, are my free choices predetermined by God?*
Because God is all-knowing, he knows how a person will freely choose before he or she actually makes the choices. But God's knowledge of our future choices does not determine those future choices. God created us with free will so that we might choose freely. In fact, "To human beings God even gives the power of freely sharing in his providence by entrusting them with the responsibility of 'subduing' the earth and having dominion over it (cf. Gen 1:26-28). God thus enables men to be intelligent and free causes in order to complete the work of creation, to perfect its harmony for their own good and that of their neighbors" (CCC 307).

9. *How can God permit evil in the world?*
God has created us with free will. This freedom has made evil possible because we are not forced to do the good. Therefore, evil is our doing, not God's. Evil is misused freedom. God permits evil in the world because he has created us to be free. He respects the freedom of his creatures and, in his infinite wisdom, is able to derive good from it. "God is in no way, directly or indirectly, the cause of moral evil" (cf. St. Augustine, *De libero arbitrio* 1,1, 2: PL 32, 1223; St. Thomas Aquinas, *STh* I-II, 79, 1) (CCC 311). The only way to obliterate evil from the world would be to remove the power of free will from the people who inhabit it. Innocent suffer-

ing, death (especially among the young), war, poverty, and disease are subject to God's providence and not easily explained. Only the Christian faith as a whole can provide a response. *"There is not a single aspect of the Christian message that is not in part an answer to the question of evil"* (CCC 309).

God does not take pleasure in the suffering his infinite wisdom and mercy allow. In the face of the incomprehensible mystery of evil, with God's grace and the redemptive suffering and death of Christ to support us, Christians trust the incomprehensible mystery of good.

10. *What does God intend for me?*

God created us to live in communion with him forever. According to St. Paul's First Letter to Timothy, "[God] wills everyone to be saved and to come to knowledge of the truth" (1 Tm 2:4). Thus, God intends the eternal salvation of all people, continually calls us to it, and provides the capacity to accept it. God's will for us respects our freedom, but our freedom does not alter God's will for us.

QUESTIONS FOR GROUP DISCUSSION

1. Why have people always believed in a god or gods?
2. How has the Christian concept of God evolved?
3. How can there be three distinct persons in one God?
4. How does my free will relate to God's providence?
5. Is God really like a super-powerful human being?
6. What is the relationship between faith and reason?
7. Does God cause bad things to happen?

QUESTIONS FOR PERSONAL REFLECTION

1. What is my image of God?
2. Do I feel that God is close to me personally?

3. How do I experience God as my Creator?

4. How do I experience God as my Savior?

5. How do I experience God as the Sanctifier of my life?

6. Does my prayer reflect my relationship with God?

PRAYER TO THE HOLY TRINITY

O my God, Trinity whom I adore, help me forget myself entirely so to establish myself in you, unmovable and peaceful as if my soul were already in eternity. May nothing be able to trouble my peace or make me leave you, O my unchanging God, but may each minute bring me more deeply into your mystery! Grant my soul peace. Make it your heaven, your beloved dwelling and the place of your rest. May I never abandon you there, but may I be there, whole and entire, completely vigilant in my faith, entirely adoring, and wholly given over to your creative action.

BLESSED ELIZABETH OF THE TRINITY

CHAPTER 4
Jesus Christ

═══

SCRIPTURE REFLECTION

In the beginning was the Word,
  and the Word was with God,
  and the Word was God.
He was in the beginning with God.
All things came to be through him,
  and without him nothing came to be.
What came to be through him was life,
  and this life was the light of the human race;
the light shines in the darkness,
  and the darkness has not overcome it.

JOHN 1:1-5

INTRODUCTION

The history of the Israelite people is a tale of oscillating fidelity and infidelity to the covenant, God's promise of his abiding love. Throughout it all, God maintained his intention to send the Messiah, the anointed one, who would redeem his people. This Messiah, however, would not be quite what the people expected. He would not be a powerful, temporal ruler who would lead the Israelite nation to world-power status. He would instead be the suffering Servant, a spiritual leader, whose power was exercised on a much deeper level than a merely political one.

We experience Jesus Christ as the central figure of the New Testament, the fulfillment of the promise of the Old Testament. In absolute obedience to the Father, he accepted his mission to suffer, to die, and to rise in order to save us. Despite temptation, he was faithful to his call, just as God's love is ever faithful to us. Jesus came primarily to announce the Kingdom of God and to proclaim our salvation from sin, suffering, and death. He made good on his Father's eternal promise to love his people with an abiding, unswerving, redemptive love. "The Spirit of the Lord is upon me, / because he has anointed me / to bring glad tidings to the poor. / He has sent me to proclaim liberty to captives / and recovery of sight to the blind, / to let the oppressed go free, / and to proclaim a year acceptable to the Lord" (Lk 4:18-19).

STUDY QUESTIONS

1. Who is Jesus?

Jesus is the eternal Son of God made man. He is the second person of the Blessed Trinity, who was conceived by the power of the Holy Spirit. He was born of a Jewish woman, the Blessed Virgin Mary, in the city of Bethlehem during the reign of King Herod and the emperor Caesar Augustus. He was a carpenter by trade. He was crucified under Pontius Pilate during the reign of the emperor Tiberius. He rose from the dead, ascended into heaven, is seated at the right hand of the Father, and is the eternal judge of the living and the dead. After his death and resurrection, Jesus was called "the Christ."

2. Why do we call Jesus "Christ"?

St. Peter's confession of faith in Jesus proclaimed, "You are the Messiah, the Son of the living God" (Mt 16:16). The word "Christ" is a Greek translation of the Hebrew word *Messiah*, which means "anointed." He was the Savior for whom Israel had longed over thousands of years. But he was more than that: he was the Savior of the world. The title "Christ" "became the name proper to Jesus only because he accomplished perfectly the divine mission that 'Christ' signifies" (CCC 436). By common usage it was appended to the name "Jesus" in order to indicate the identification of Jesus with his mission.

3. Basically, what do Christians believe about Jesus Christ?

Christians believe that Jesus Christ is the second divine person of the Blessed Trinity. He is the only and eternal Son of God and Savior of the world. We believe that he is at once for all time both fully divine and fully human and that his divinity and humanity are united in one divine person. In Christ, God became man. "Jesus Christ possesses two natures, one divine and the other human, not confused, but united in the one person of God's Son" (CCC 481). We believe that Jesus Christ was conceived by the power of the Holy Spirit in the womb of a virgin, Mary, without the intervention of a human father. We believe that he suffered, died, was raised from the dead, and ascended into heaven so that we might share his divine life. We believe that he is the judge of all humankind and history, just as he is their Savior. The action of God in Jesus Christ is responsible for the salvation of the world.

4. Is Jesus Christ really human?

"The unique and altogether singular event of the Incarnation of the Son of God does not mean that Jesus Christ is part God and part man, nor does it imply that he is the result of a confused mixture of the divine and the human. He became truly man while remaining truly God" (CCC 464). In the mystery of the Incarnation, Jesus Christ, the only Son of God, became human flesh through the power of the Holy Spirit and assumed human nature without losing his divine nature. Jesus Christ is really human. He has a human body and human soul, with its operations of intellect and will. He is really human, not only because he is a historical person who actually lived on this earth, but also because he experienced the wide spectrum of human emotions that are common among human beings. He developed as other humans do. Jesus is not God pretending to be human.

"The Son of God ... worked with human hands; he thought with a human mind. He acted with a human will, and with a human heart he loved. Born of the Virgin Mary, he has truly been made one of us, like to us in all things except sin" (*Pastoral Constitution on the Church in the Modern World*, 22). Jesus shared our life in order to enable us to share his divine life.

5. *Is Jesus Christ really divine?*

Jesus Christ is really divine, co-eternal with the Father and the Holy Spirit. His divinity cannot be proven through a series of logical propositions because his divinity is a mystery of faith and, therefore, the truth revealed by God, the source of all truth. Jesus is described in the New Testament as "Lord," as having an intimate relationship with the Father, and as the eternal Son of God. In the early creedal statements of the Church, he is referred to as the Word of God made Flesh, God from God, Light from Light, true God from true God. Jesus is not man trying to be God. "Jesus Christ is true God and true man, in the unity of his divine person; for this reason he is the one and only mediator between God and men" (CCC 480).

6. *How could Jesus Christ have been born of a virgin?*

The virginal conception of Jesus Christ refers to the belief that he was conceived in the womb of the Virgin Mary without the intervention of a human father. The virginal conception of Jesus bears witness to his divinity, since God alone is his Father. "From all eternity God chose for the mother of his Son a daughter of Israel, a young Jewish woman of Nazareth in Galilee" (CCC 488). By a singular grace, God prepared the Virgin Mary to be the mother of his only Son. He preserved her, from the moment of her conception in the womb of her mother, from every stain of sin. "From the first formulations of her faith, the Church has confessed that Jesus was conceived solely by the power of the Holy Spirit in the womb of the Virgin Mary" (CCC 496). The Church also confesses that Mary remained a virgin for the length of her life.

7. Did Jesus Christ really die?

The actual physical death of Jesus Christ is properly recorded and attested to by the competent civil authorities of the time, as well as by the testimony of his own disciples. Jesus did not pretend to die or seem to die, nor was he replaced by a stand-in. Jesus really died. "To the benefit of every man, Jesus Christ tasted death (cf. Heb 2:9). It is truly the Son of God made man who died and was buried" (CCC 629).

8. Why did Jesus Christ die?

" 'Christ died for our sins in accordance with the scriptures' (1 Cor 15:3)" (CCC 619). On the surface, Jesus was executed because religious and political leaders of the time saw in him a real threat to their respective established orders. The deeper reason for Christ's journey to Jerusalem and his acceptance of death was to embrace the will of his Father in the ultimate act of creative love. Jesus freely accepted death in order to redeem us from the bondage of sin, not because of any vindictive need on the part of the Father, but precisely because of his love, a love that frees us from the domination of sin, suffering, and death. "Our salvation flows from God's initiative of love for us, because 'he loved us and sent his Son to be the expiation for our sins' (1 Jn 4:10)" (CCC 620). Jesus Christ freely offered himself for our salvation. By dying he destroyed our death.

9. Did Jesus Christ really rise from the dead?

The resurrection of Jesus Christ, not his temporary resuscitation, is central to the Christian faith. There are no eyewitnesses to the actual event of the Resurrection itself. The tomb in which he was laid was found empty, his disciples saw the risen Jesus in the flesh, and his followers were clearly transformed by their experience. Jesus entered a new kind of experience through the Resurrection, which he pledges that we too will share. "Faith in the Resurrection has as its object an event which is historically attested to by the disciples, who really encountered the Risen One. At the same time, this event is mysteriously transcendent insofar as it is the entry of Christ's humanity into the glory of God" (CCC 656).

10. Why did Jesus Christ rise from the dead?

Jesus Christ rose from the dead for the same reason that he died on the cross — namely, to save us. The death and resurrection of Jesus should be looked upon as two elements of the same reality, the redemption of humankind. The Resurrection is the decisive event for the Christian. It confirms all of Christ's works and teachings and verifies his divinity. "Christ, 'the first born from the dead' (Col 1:18), is the principle of our own resurrection, even now by the justification of our souls (cf. Rom 6:4), and one day by the new life he will impart to our bodies (cf. Rom 8:11)" (CCC 658). By rising he restored our life.

11. How is Jesus Christ our Redeemer?

Jesus Christ is our Redeemer because he sacrificed his life for our salvation. The life of Jesus Christ, which culminates in his death and resurrection, is an act of love — the ultimate act of love. "By his loving obedience to the Father, 'unto death, even death on a cross' (Phil 2:8), Jesus fulfills the atoning mission (cf. Isa 53:10) of the suffering Servant, who will 'make many righteous; and he shall bear their iniquities' (Isa 53:11; cf. Rom 5:19)" (CCC 623). Christ's sacrifice stands opposed to the forces of evil, hatred, greed, manipulation, oppression, and fear. It breaks the domination of humankind by sin, suffering, and death, and it frees us to life in Christ. Thus we are redeemed.

12. Where did Jesus Christ go after the Resurrection?

The followers of Jesus experienced the presence of the risen Lord for some time after the Resurrection and then underwent a dramatic separation from him that is memorialized in the Ascension of the Lord into heaven. The doctrine of the Ascension states that Jesus was raised to the right hand of the Father, the place of the glory and honor of divinity, from where he judges humankind and history. "Christ's ascension marks the definitive entrance of Jesus' humanity into God's heavenly domain, whence he will come again (cf. Acts 1:11)" (CCC 665). It also clearly places the responsibility for proclaiming the nearness of the Kingdom of God squarely on the shoulders of the followers of Jesus, who, empowered by the Holy Spirit, are his presence in the world.

13. How is Jesus Christ present today?

Jesus Christ is present today in the Church. "As Lord, Christ is also head of the Church, which is his Body (cf. Eph 1:22). Taken up to heaven and glorified after he had thus fully accomplished his mission, Christ dwells on earth in his Church" (CCC 669). Christ is present when the Gospel is preached boldly and assimilated into the life of the community. He is present in the Eucharist, under the appearances of bread and wine; in the proclamation of the Word; in the person of the priest; and in the assembly. He is present through the power and movement of the Holy Spirit, who unites and animates the Church as it extends itself into history. Jesus Christ is therefore present in word, in sacrament, and in Spirit.

14. Is Jesus Christ going to return?

Since his ascension, the Church has been anticipating the second and final coming of Christ, even though the time and manner of his return are not known. His final coming will be the completion of human history and the fulfillment of human destiny. "On Judgment Day at the end of the world, Christ will come in glory to achieve the definitive triumph of good over evil" (CCC 681). The whole of the Christian message is, therefore, cast in the context of a hopeful longing for the Lord's return. "That is why Christians pray, above all in the Eucharist, to hasten Christ's return by saying to him (cf. 1 Cor 11:26; 2 Pet 3:11-12): *Marana tha!* 'Our Lord, come!' (1 Cor 16:22; Rev 22:17, 20)" (CCC 671).

QUESTIONS FOR GROUP DISCUSSION

1. How is Jesus Christ fully human?
2. How is Jesus Christ truly divine?
3. Why do we hold Mary in such great esteem?
4. Why did Jesus Christ accept death?
5. Why is the resurrection of Jesus Christ so important for Christians?

QUESTIONS FOR PERSONAL REFLECTION

1. In the life of Christ, what holds the most meaning for me?
2. What characteristic do I admire most in Jesus Christ?
3. How ready am I to bring about a change of heart in myself?
4. How does the fact that God became man affect me and my attitude toward others?
5. Is the resurrection of Jesus Christ a source of hope for me?

PRAYER FOR PROTECTION

Against all Satan's spells and wiles,
Against false words of heresy,
Against the knowledge that defiles,
Against the heart's idolatry,
Against the wizard's evil craft,
Against the death-wound and the burning,
the choking wave, the poisoned shaft,
protect me, Christ, till thy returning.
Christ be with me, Christ within me,
Christ behind me, Christ before me,
Christ beside me, Christ to win me,
Christ to comfort and restore me,
Christ beneath me, Christ above me,
Christ in quiet, Christ in danger,
Christ in the hearts of all that love me,
Christ in the mouth of friend and stranger.

FROM THE BREASTPLATE OF ST. PATRICK

CHAPTER 5
The Holy Spirit

———

SCRIPTURE REFLECTION

"If you love me, you will keep my commandments. And I will ask the Father, and he will give you another Advocate to be with you always, the Spirit of truth, which the world cannot accept, because it neither sees nor knows it. But you know it, because it remains with you, and will be in you."

JOHN 14:15-17

INTRODUCTION

Jesus' parting gift to his disciples was his own Spirit. He promised them that he would not leave them alone but would send them the Holy Spirit, who "will teach you everything and remind you of all that [I] told you" (Jn 14:26). The Church celebrates this coming of the Holy Spirit at Pentecost, originally a Jewish harvest festival marking the fiftieth day after Passover and celebrating God's covenant with Moses.

The Holy Spirit is present both to the individual person and to the whole Church. The personal presence of the Holy Spirit is referred to when Jesus says, "Whoever loves me will keep my word, and my Father will love him, and we will come to him and make our dwelling with him" (Jn 14:23). The presence of the Holy Spirit on a most intimate level is God's own life and love vibrant within a person. St. Paul says,

"The love of God has been poured out into our hearts through the holy Spirit that has been given to us" (Rom 5:5).

The Holy Spirit is present to the Church as its life force. Jesus refers to the Holy Spirit as an advocate for his mission to proclaim the Kingdom of God, an advocate who enables the disciples to bear witness to Jesus in the world and to form a community of love in the world. This movement outward from Jerusalem to the ends of the earth assures the Church's growth precisely because of the Spirit's presence within it.

STUDY QUESTIONS

1. **Who is the Holy Spirit?**

" 'Holy Spirit' is the proper name of the one whom we adore and glorify with the Father and the Son" (CCC 691). Jesus called the Holy Spirit the "Advocate," the "Paraclete," and the "Spirit of Truth." St. Paul called him the "Spirit of the promise," the "Spirit of adoption," the "Spirit of Christ," the "Spirit of the Lord," and the "Spirit of God." The Holy Spirit is the third divine person of the Blessed Trinity. He is a distinct person who shares equally the same, single divine being in eternal unity with the Father and the Son. The Holy Spirit is "the Lord, the giver of life, who proceeds from the Father and the Son" (Nicene Creed). The Holy Spirit is the loving bond of unity between the Father and the Son in the Blessed Trinity.

2. **What does the Holy Spirit do?**

"From the beginning to the end of time, whenever God sends his Son, he always sends his Spirit: their mission is conjoined and inseparable" (CCC 743). Since the Holy Spirit is God's gift of divine love, he is active as a constant, loving presence in the world. The Spirit's love enlightens, inspires, initiates, and enables the missionary activity of the Church. The Holy Spirit's love is also directed to each individual Christian for the purpose of leading us in a life of charity. "The Holy Spirit is at work with the Father and the Son from the beginning to the completion of the plan for our salvation" (CCC 686).

3. *How is the Holy Spirit at work in the Church?*
On the day of Pentecost, Christ fulfilled his promise by pouring out the Holy Spirit on his apostles and establishing the Church. On that day the Holy Trinity was fully revealed and the time of the Church was inaugurated. "The mission of Christ and the Holy Spirit is brought to completion in the Church, which is the Body of Christ and the Temple of the Holy Spirit.... The Spirit *prepares* men and goes out to them with his grace, in order to draw them to Christ. The Spirit *manifests* the risen Lord to them, recalls his word to them and opens their minds to the understanding of his Death and Resurrection. He *makes present* the mystery of Christ, supremely in the Eucharist, in order to reconcile them, to *bring them into communion* with God, that they may 'bear much fruit' (Jn 15:8, 16)" (CCC 737).

The Church's mission is the sacrament of the one mission of Christ and the Holy Spirit. Christ bestows his Spirit on the members of his Body, the Church, so that they go to the ends of the earth, make disciples, teach in his name, and celebrate the sacraments until he comes again. The Holy Spirit is the vital principle and source of the Christian moral life, the new life in Christ. "The Holy Spirit, the artisan of God's works, is the master of prayer" (CCC 741).

4. *How do we experience the gift of the Holy Spirit?*
God is love, and his first gift to us is himself. "The love of God has been poured out into our hearts through the holy Spirit that has been given to us" (Rom 5:5). The Holy Spirit makes us sharers in God's own life, the life of the Holy Trinity. He conforms us to the divine image. When we sin, the Holy Spirit restores us to life in

Christ. The Holy Spirit illumines our minds toward a deeper understanding of God because, by the gift of the Holy Spirit, God dwells within us. He inspires and assists us in building up the Body of Christ, the Church. He guides our decisions, choices, and judgments in the practical situations of daily living. "By this power of the Spirit, God's children can bear much fruit. He who has grafted us onto the true vine will make us bear 'the fruit of the Spirit: ... love, joy, peace, patience, kindness, goodness, faithfulness, gentleness, self-control' (Gal 5:22-23)" (CCC 736).

5. *What are the gifts of the Holy Spirit?*

Broadly speaking, every good thought or act is a gift of the Holy Spirit. In particular, the Church has traditionally enumerated seven gifts of the Holy Spirit. They are: *wisdom* to know the things of God, *understanding* to know the truth, *counsel* to know what is right, *courage* to do what is right, *knowledge* to grow in faith, *piety* to worship in faith, and a sense of *wonder and awe* to know God's power. "The moral life of Christians is sustained by the gifts of the Holy Spirit. These are permanent dispositions which make man docile in following the promptings of the Holy Spirit" (CCC 1830). In addition to the gifts of the Holy Spirit, he also cultivates certain fruits in us.

6. *What are the fruits of the Holy Spirit?*

"The *fruits* of the Spirit are perfections that the Holy Spirit forms in us as the first fruits of eternal glory. The tradition of the Church lists twelve of them: 'charity, joy, peace, patience, kindness, goodness, generosity, gentleness, faithfulness, modesty, self-control, chastity' (Gal 5:22-23 [Vulg.])" (CCC 1832).

QUESTIONS FOR GROUP DISCUSSION

1. How can the Holy Spirit be a distinct person of the Blessed Trinity and yet be united in one God?

2. In what way does the Holy Spirit direct the mission of the Church?

3. In what way does the Holy Spirit inspire an individual person?

4. What is the relationship of the Holy Spirit to God's grace?

5. Does God love us because we are good, or are we good because he loves us?

QUESTIONS FOR PERSONAL REFLECTION

1. How do I experience the presence of the Holy Spirit in my life?

2. Do I allow the Holy Spirit to transform me?

3. Are the gifts of the Holy Spirit realities in my life?

4. What are my "special" gifts?

5. How do I build up the Body of Christ?

PRAYER TO THE HOLY SPIRIT

Leader: Come, Holy Spirit.

Response: Fill the hearts of your faithful and enkindle within them the fire of your love.

Leader: Send forth your Spirit, and they shall be created.

Response: And you shall renew the face of the earth.

Leader: Let us pray.

All: O God, you have instructed the hearts of the faithful by the light of the Holy Spirit. Grant that through the same Holy Spirit we may always be truly wise and rejoice in his consolation. Through Christ our Lord. Amen.

CHAPTER 6
Sacred Scripture

SCRIPTURE REFLECTION

Since many have undertaken to compile a narrative of the events that have been fulfilled among us, just as those who were eyewitnesses from the beginning and ministers of the word have handed them down to us, I too have decided, after investigating everything accurately anew, to write it down in an orderly sequence for you, most excellent Theophilus, so that you may realize the certainty of the teachings you have received.

LUKE 1:1-4

INTRODUCTION

Today people are hungry for the authentic Word of God. We long to know what God has to say to us through the events of salvation history. We long to know what Jesus really said and did during his earthly life. We long to know the significance of his saving actions for our lives.

Today, Bible-study groups are very popular settings for adult learners, and Scripture-study programs are among the best-sellers of religious publications. Scriptural reflection as a basis for personal and shared prayer is quickly becoming a regular part of adult faith-formation programs. Catholic people consistently expect homilists to relate the Word of God to their daily lives. They are disappointed when they do not feel as nourished by the sacrament of the Word as they are by the sacrament of the Eucharist.

Bible-based preachers and television evangelists have had a powerful influence in many people's lives, especially in the past ten years. Catholics hear them offer simplistic biblical quotations out of context in response to some of their own most troublesome questions. At first these quotations seem satisfying solutions, but most often they do not ring true. They hold out a certainty, however, that is very attractive. Perhaps we are so often confused and frustrated by the events of our own times, by the complexity of our lives, by the difficult decisions we face, and by our apparent lack of control that we seek peace and tranquillity in the solutions of a simpler age.

Sacred Scripture, however, is neither a neatly wrapped package of well-defined doctrines nor a road map for Christian living. Biblical texts cannot be used to prove certain teachings, for not all of the Church teachings are rooted in Scripture. "The Christian faith is not a 'religion of the book.' Christianity is the religion of the 'Word' of God, a word which is 'not a written and mute word, but the Word which is incarnate and living' (St. Bernard, *S. missus est hom.* 4, 11: PL 183, 86)" (CCC 108). Together with Tradition, Sacred Scripture forms the living Word of God, which has been handed on from one generation to another and which continually nourishes the life of the Church. As the *Dogmatic Constitution on Divine Revelation* states:

> All the preaching of the Church must be nourished and regulated by Sacred Scripture. For in the sacred books, the Father who is in heaven meets his children with great love and speaks with them; and the force and the power in the Word of God is so great that it stands as the support and energy of the Church, the strength of faith for her [children], the food of the soul, the pure and everlasting source of spiritual life [n. 21].

STUDY QUESTIONS

1. *What is Sacred Scripture?*

Sacred Scripture, or the Bible, contains the Word of God, Jesus Christ. "Through all the words of Sacred Scripture, God speaks only one single Word, his one Utterance in whom he expresses himself completely" (cf. Heb 1:1-3) (CCC 102). Sacred Scripture is a collection of books that hold the truth of God's revelation. These books were inspired by the Holy Spirit and composed by human authors. The Bible is the written record of God's action in salvation history. It forms, enables, nourishes, and strengthens the Church.

2. *How is the Bible divided?*

"It was by the apostolic Tradition that the Church discerned which writings are to be included in the list of the sacred books (cf. *DV* 8 § 3). This complete list is called the canon of Scripture" (CCC 120). There are 73 books contained in the Bible. It is divided into two sections: the Old Testament (46 books) and the New Testament (27 books). The word "testament" means covenant or agreement.

3. *What is the Old Testament?*

The Old Testament is an anthology of historical books that recorded the experiences of the Israelite people, instructional books that codified their moral and liturgical practices, prophetic books that announced the messages God revealed to the prophets who rose up from the Israelite people, and wisdom books that contained the prudent advice of the sages among them. Essentially, the Old Testament records the history of salvation from creation through the old covenant with Israel. It describes God's divine direction of human history and the historical development of the Israelite people's understanding of God.

The writings of the Old Testament "are a storehouse of sublime teaching on God and of sound wisdom on human life, as well as a wonderful treasury of prayers; in them, too, the mystery of our salvation is present in a hidden way" (*Dogmatic Constitution on Divine Revelation*, 15). For the most part, the books of the Old Testament were written in the Hebrew language between 900 B.C. and 160 B.C.

4. What is the New Testament?

The New Testament consists of the four Gospels, or announcements of the Good News of Jesus, written by Mark, Matthew, Luke, and John; the Acts of the Apostles written by Luke; the letters that Paul wrote to early Christian communities; other letters addressed to the whole Church; and the book of Revelation, a message of hope for Christians being persecuted in Rome. The central object of the New Testament "is Jesus Christ, God's incarnate Son: his acts, teachings, Passion and glorification, and his Church's beginnings under the Spirit's guidance" (cf. *DV* 20) (CCC 124). The books of the New Testament were written in Greek between A.D. 50 and approximately A.D. 135.

5. Who wrote the Bible?

God is the author of Sacred Scripture. The truths contained in Sacred Scripture were written down by human authors under the inspiration of the Holy Spirit. The Holy Spirit guided human authors to write what he wanted to communicate. However, the human authors were not merely passive instruments. Though the Holy Spirit acted in and through them, the human authors used the abilities, language, and style reflective of their respective historical situation to express the Word of God that was revealed to them. "Since therefore all that the inspired authors or sacred writers affirm should be regarded as affirmed by the Holy Spirit, we must acknowledge that the books of Scripture firmly, faithfully, and without error teach that truth which God, for the sake of our salvation, wished to see confided to the Sacred Scriptures" (*Dogmatic Constitution on Divine Revelation*, 11).

6. Is everything in the Bible true?

Yes, everything in the Bible is true. "The inspired books teach the truth" (CCC 107). The human authors recorded free from error the truth God wanted to communicate. God intended to communicate the truth of his plan and purpose for creation, the ultimate meaning of life. God did not intend, however, to impart scientific facts. The human authors used the material available at their specific time in history and the popular literary forms of their particular ages to communicate a message for all times. The inaccuracy of certain scientific data used by the human authors more than 3,000 years ago to communicate divine truths does not reduce the reliability of those truths.

7. What is a literary form?

A literary form is a specific structure for written communication. Histories, instructions, legends, songs, poems, dreams, dramas, myths, proverbs, allegories, prophecies, gospels, parables, letters, and apocalypses are all literary forms that are found in Sacred Scripture. Each literary form communicates meaning and truth in a manner unique to the particular form. For example, both poems and letters in the Bible communicate truth, but in very different ways. In order to begin to understand the truth that God intends to communicate through the literary form, it is necessary to have a sense of the literary form itself.

8. How does one interpret Sacred Scripture?

The individual always brings personal faith and experience to his or her interpretation of the Bible. But one's thoughts and feelings about the meaning of the Bible always need to be evaluated in light of the Church's tradition and teachings. Biblical scholarship has enhanced the Church's understanding of the Bible greatly, especially in the last 50 years. Most Catholic Bibles provide good introductions to each of the books and helpful footnotes and references. These introductions and footnotes should be carefully noted as one reads the Bible, as they are extremely important aids for accurate interpretation of its meaning. "Since God speaks in Sacred Scripture through men in human fashion, the interpreter of Sacred Scripture, in order to see clearly what God wanted to communicate to us, should carefully investigate what meaning the sacred writers really intended, and what God wanted to manifest by means of their words" (*Dogmatic Constitution on Divine Revelation*, 12).

9. *Are there inconsistencies in Sacred Scripture?*

Yes. For example, in Matthew's account of the Lord's Prayer, there are four petitions; in Luke's there are only three. In Matthew's account of the Beatitudes, there are eight blessings; in Luke's there are four blessings and four warnings. These editorial inconsistencies could reflect the individual character of each biblical author, the source used by the author, or the specific purpose or theme the author is attempting to communicate. The accounts of Paul's conversion in Acts are different from those given in his own letter to the Galatians. Such differences are usually the result of historical, cultural, or linguistic limitations necessarily imposed on any human author.

10. *How were the books of the Bible gathered together?*

The books of the Bible were written over a period of more than 1,000 years. A Greek translation of the existing books of the Old Testament was made about A.D. 300. Other sacred writings judged by Church authorities to be worthy and authentic were added over the following century. The need to preserve the sacred New Testament writings was not felt until the death of the last of the eyewitnesses to the public ministry of Jesus. Writings of apostolic origin were placed in a special category. "The *Gospels* are the heart of all the Scriptures 'because they are our principal source for the life and teaching of the Incarnate Word, our Savior' (*DV* 18)" (CCC 125). By the end of the fourth century, the canon, or list of sacred writings, was determined by the Church authorities.

11. *How should one use Sacred Scripture?*

One should read the Bible with faith and in the context of prayer, for God speaks to us through the words of Sacred Scripture. This is the ancient practice of the Church called *lectio divina*. The *Dogmatic Constitution on Divine Revelation* teaches, "The sacred synod ... urges all the Christian faithful ... to learn by frequent reading of the divine Scriptures 'the excellent knowledge of Jesus Christ' (Phil 3:8). 'For ignorance of the Scriptures is ignorance of Christ.' ... And let them remember that prayer should accompany the reading of Sacred Scripture, so that God and man may talk together" (n. 25). One should study Sacred Scripture with the careful direction of trained leaders and approved support materials, for the layers of meaning in the stories of the Bible are innumerable and sometimes difficult to understand.

The truth of Sacred Scripture is for all people of all ages. It reminds us of God's loving and saving presence throughout human history. It reminds us of God's involvement in our lives today and of the divine assistance in the here and now.

12. *How does the Church use Sacred Scripture?*

In the Church's celebration of the Eucharistic liturgy, readings from Sacred Scripture comprise the center of the Liturgy of the Word. In fact, selections from Sacred Scripture are essential elements of the celebration of all the sacraments. The Psalms especially are significant parts of the official daily prayer of the Church, the Liturgy of the Hours. The study of Sacred Scripture should be the very soul of the Church's theology. The Church's ministry of the Word — pastoral preaching, catechetics, all types of Christian formation and evangelization — is inspired and nourished by Sacred Scripture. Sacred Scripture prompts, animates, and sustains the entire prayer life of the community of the faithful. It provides "strength for their faith, food for the soul, and a pure and lasting font of spiritual life" (*Dogmatic Constitution on Divine Revelation*, 21).

QUESTIONS FOR GROUP DISCUSSION

1. What is the oral tradition?
2. Are Catholics supposed to believe everything they read in the Bible?
3. What translations of Sacred Scripture are recommended?
4. How is Sacred Scripture used in the liturgy and life of the Church?
5. How can something be true and yet not scientifically factual?
6. If God is the principal author of Sacred Scripture, how can there be inconsistencies?

QUESTIONS FOR PERSONAL REFLECTION

1. Do I own a Bible?
2. Is my Bible displayed in a prominent place in my home?
3. Do I read parts of Sacred Scripture on my own?
4. Do I listen attentively when the readings are proclaimed at Mass?
5. Do I share my thoughts and feelings on the meaning of scriptural passages with others?
6. Would I like to join a Bible-study group?

Leader: Spirit of Truth, present everywhere and filling all things, treasure of all good and source of life, come dwell in us and form us in the Word made flesh, Jesus Christ, who lives with you and the Father in the unity of love and peace.

Reader: A reading from the Acts of the Apostles.

Then the angel of the Lord spoke to Philip, "Get up and head south on the road that goes down from Jerusalem to Gaza, the desert route." So he got up and set out. Now there was an Ethiopian eunuch, a court official of the Candace, that is, the queen of the Ethiopians, in charge of her entire treasury, who had come to Jerusalem to worship, and was returning home. Seated in his chariot, he was reading the prophet Isaiah. The Spirit said to Philip, "Go and join up with that chariot." Philip ran up and heard him reading Isaiah the prophet and said, "Do you understand what you are reading?" He replied, "How can I, unless someone instructs me?" So he invited Philip to get in and sit with him. This was the scripture passage he was reading:

"Like a sheep he was led to the slaughter,
    and as a lamb before its shearer is silent,
        so he opened not his mouth.
In [his] humiliation justice was denied him.
    Who will tell of his posterity?
        For his life is taken from the earth."

Then the eunuch said to Philip in reply, "I beg you, about whom is the prophet saying this? About himself, or about someone else?" Then Philip opened his mouth and, beginning with this scripture passage, he proclaimed Jesus to him. As they traveled along the

---

road they came to some water, and the eunuch said, "Look, there is water. What is to prevent my being baptized?" Then he ordered the chariot to stop, and Philip and the eunuch both went down into the water, and he baptized him. When they came out of the water, the Spirit of the Lord snatched Philip away, and the eunuch saw him no more, but continued on his way rejoicing.

ACTS 8:26-39

Leader: *To each invocation please respond, "Lord, form us in your Word."*

> *In our zeal to see your face ...*
> *When we wander in the desert ...*
> *When we are lost and abandoned ...*
> *As we long to know your name ...*
> *When we hear you calling in the night ...*
> *As our faith and confidence weakens ...*
> *Throughout the length of our journey home ...*

Leader: *Gracious God, we place the longings of our hearts before you. Listen to the words we speak, and quiet our murmurings to receive your Word, Jesus Christ. We ask this in his name.*
All: *Amen.*
Leader: *May the Lord bless you and keep you. May his face shine upon you, and be gracious to you. May he look upon you with kindness, and give you his peace.*
All: *Amen.*

CHAPTER 7

The Church

SCRIPTURE REFLECTION

Awe came upon everyone, and many wonders and signs were done through the apostles. All who believed were together and had all things in common; they would sell their property and possessions and divide them among all according to each one's need. Every day they devoted themselves to meeting together in the temple area and to breaking bread in their homes. They ate their meals with exultation and sincerity of heart, praising God and enjoying favor with all the people. And every day the Lord added to their number those who were being saved.

ACTS 2:43-47

INTRODUCTION

Ordinarily, Christian people experience the Church as a local community of believers who gather to express their faith together in word, in service, and in worship. "They devoted themselves to the teaching of the apostles and to the communal life, to the breaking of the bread and to the prayers" (Acts 2:42). As the Church celebrates the memory of the Lord Jesus, her identity is at once set forth and made more firm. St. Paul described the Church as the "Body of Christ" to stress that the Church is an organism whose parts are related and even dependent one upon the other. In his first letter to the Church of Corinth he says:

As a body is one though it has many parts, and all the parts of the body, though many, are one body, so also Christ. For in one Spirit we were all baptized into one body, whether Jews or Greeks, slaves or free persons, and we were all given to drink of one Spirit.

Now the body is not a single part, but many.... If [one] part suffers, all the parts suffer with it; if one part is honored, all the parts share its joy.

Now you are Christ's body, and individually parts of it [1 Cor 12:12-14, 26-27].

It is important for us to realize that the Church is a pilgrim people, a people on a journey of faith. We have not yet reached our goal but rather are on our way. We are sinners, weak and vulnerable, growing into the fullness that is the Body of Christ. There is a clear sense, then, that all are welcome, that all belong.

Local parishes provide the opportunity for people to feel a sense of community, belonging, and welcome. Every follower of the Lord is called upon by his or her baptismal commitment to bear witness to Jesus to others, for the Church discloses the Kingdom of God to the world. We are the ones who show others how to be a loving people, dedicated to justice and united by faith. In his Letter to the Ephesians St. Paul says:

[Strive] to preserve the unity of the spirit through the bond of peace: one body and one Spirit, as you were also called to the one hope of your call; one Lord, one faith, one baptism; one God and Father of all, who is over all and through all and in all [Eph 4:3-6].

STUDY QUESTIONS

1. What is the Church?

The Church is the assembly of those called by God from the ends of the earth to form "a chosen race, a royal priesthood, a holy nation, a people set apart" (Preface of Sundays in Ordinary Time I; cf. 1 Pt 2:9). The Church draws her life from the incarnate Word of God, Jesus Christ, and from his Body and Blood in the Eucharist. The Church is both the means and the goal of God's loving plan of goodness. She is the sacrament of salvation in this world and the instrument of the communion of God and humankind. The Church is the Body of Christ in the world, with Christ as her head and the Holy Spirit as her soul. She is the Bride of Christ in that he loved her and handed himself over for her. She is the Temple of the Holy Spirit. "The Church is both visible and spiritual, a hierarchical society and the Mystical Body of Christ. She is one, yet formed of two components, human and divine. That is her mystery, which only faith can accept" (CCC 779).

2. *Who belongs to the Church?*

Those who confess the Lordship of Jesus Christ, who ratify that faith in Baptism and in the sacramental life of the Church, who accept all the means of salvation given to the Church by Christ, and who embrace the ecclesiastical organization of the Church are fully incorporated into the Church of Christ, which subsists in the Catholic Church. This is not to say that other people cannot be holy, that other people cannot worship God or that other people cannot be saved. Members of the Orthodox churches are in close, but not full, communion with the Catholic Church. The Church is joined in many ways to those who have been baptized but who do not profess the Catholic faith in its entirety or who have not preserved the unity Christ willed for his Church. Those who believe in Christ but who have not been properly baptized experience imperfect communion with the Church.

The Church has a special bond with the Jewish people since they were the first to hear the Word of God, and their faith is a response to the God's revelation in the Old Testament. The Church also has a special link with Muslims since they profess to hold the faith of Abraham and worship the one true God. "The Catholic Church recognizes in other religions that search, among shadows and images, for the God who is unknown yet near since he gives life and breath and all things and wants all men to be saved. Thus, the Church considers all goodness and truth found in these religions as 'a preparation for the Gospel and given by him who enlightens all men that they may at length have life' (*LG* 16; cf. *NA* 2; *EN* 53)" (CCC 843).

3. *Do you have to belong to the Church in order to be saved?*

God wills salvation for all people. All who seek God and do his will can be saved. Church membership does not guarantee salvation, but "all salvation comes from Christ the Head through the Church which is his Body" (CCC 846). The Second Vatican Council teaches "that the Church, a pilgrim now on earth, is necessary for salvation: the one Christ is the mediator and the way of salvation; he is present to us in his body which is the Church. He himself explicitly asserted the necessity of faith and Baptism, and thereby affirmed at the same time the necessity of the Church which men enter through Baptism as through a door. Hence they could not be saved who, knowing that the Catholic Church was founded as necessary by God through Christ, would refuse either to enter it or to remain in it" (*Dogmatic Constitution on the Church*, 14).

4. *Who established the Church?*

In order to accomplish his Father's loving plan of salvation, Jesus Christ instituted the Church. He first announced the coming of the Kingdom of God. He gathered his disciples around him, instructed them, and sent his Spirit to guide them. They became the seed of the Kingdom of God already present in the mystery of the Church. Christ empowered his disciples to continue his mission and to announce the coming of the Kingdom to the ends of the earth. "The Lord Jesus endowed his community with a structure that will remain until the Kingdom is fully achieved" (CCC 765). In this way Jesus established the Church as the institution from which the Kingdom of God springs forth on earth.

5. *How was the early Church organized?*

The organizational structure of the Church developed gradually. From the beginning, Christ was head of the Church. The Church was born of his self-sacrifice for our salvation. He is the source of her authority and mission, her gifts and ministries. From a number of disciples, Jesus chose twelve whom he called "apostles." They are the foundation stones of the Church. These he prepared for leadership roles within the community of believers. "To proclaim the faith and plant his reign, Christ sends his apostles and their successors. He gives them a share in his own mission. From him they receive the power to act in his person" (CCC 935).

6. *Did Peter have a special role?*

Jesus entrusted Peter with his own ministry in a special way. Jesus told him three times to shepherd his flock. Peter is always mentioned first among the apostles and was looked to as their leader. He was the chief spokesman for the early Church. "The Lord made Simon alone, whom he named Peter, the 'rock' of his Church. He gave him the keys of his Church and instituted him shepherd of the whole flock" (cf. Mt 16:18–19; Jn 21:15-17) (CCC 881).

7. *Who governs the Catholic Church?*

Jesus Christ is the head of the Church; his Spirit directs the efforts of the Church. Christ handed on his authority to his apostles and their successors, the bishops. Thus, the bishops of the Church, by the laying on of hands, have the responsibility of guiding, protecting, and leading the People of God. As bishop of the Church of Rome, the Pope is the head of the college of bishops and, as such, holds full authority over the whole Church. The Pope and the college of bishops are not two opposing tensions in the exercise of authority. Authority in the Church is pastoral service — that is, a work of unselfish love exercised with diligent care. "This pastoral office of Peter and the other apostles belongs to the Church's very foundation and is continued by the bishops under the primacy of the Pope" (CCC 881).

8. *What is a bishop?*

In order that Christ's mission might continue after their death, the apostles designated certain men as their successors and handed on to them the duty of tending the flock of Christ. A bishop is a successor to the apostles. He is the shepherd of the local Church that has been entrusted to him by the Pope. He is the visible source and foundation of the unity of the local Church. A bishop is one who has received the fullness of the sacrament of Holy Orders. Together with all other bishops, he belongs to the college of bishops, who care for the whole Church. "Helped by the priests, their co-workers, and by the deacons, the bishops have the duty of authentically teaching the faith, celebrating divine worship, above all the Eucharist, and guiding their Churches as true pastors. Their responsibility also includes concern for all the Churches, with and under the Pope" (CCC 939).

9. *How are bishops chosen?*

Bishops are chosen by the Pope from the recommendations of other bishops. In most cases bishops seek the counsel of selected clergy, religious, and laity in making such recommendations.

10. *What is the Pope?*

"The bishop of the Church of Rome, successor to St. Peter, is 'head of the college of bishops, the Vicar of Christ and Pastor of the universal Church on earth' (CIC, can. 331)" (CCC 936). He is the leader of the Church throughout the world. He is the visible sign and center of unity in the whole Church. By divine institution, the

Pope "enjoys supreme, full, immediate and universal power in the care of souls" (*Decree on the Pastoral Office of Bishops in the Church*, 2). In matters of faith and morals, when he is specifically exercising his office, the Pope is infallible.

11. How is the Pope chosen?

When a Pope dies, the College of Cardinals (specially chosen bishops from all over the world) gather in solemn conclave to elect a successor. They vote by secret ballot until two-thirds of the cardinals agree on the new Pope. For the past several hundred years, the College of Cardinals has chosen one of their own number as Pope.

12. What is infallibility?

"In order to preserve the Church in the purity of the faith handed on by the apostles, Christ who is the Truth willed to confer on her a share in his own infallibility. By a 'supernatural sense of faith' the People of God, under the guidance of the Church's living Magisterium, 'unfailingly adheres to this faith' (*LG* 12; cf. *DV* 10)" (CCC 889).

Infallibility is the gift of the Holy Spirit to the Church whereby the Pope and the bishops in communion with him are preserved from error when they proclaim a doctrine of faith or morals that is to be believed by all the faithful. "The Roman Pontiff, head of the college of bishops, enjoys this infallibility in virtue of his office, when, as supreme pastor and teacher of all the faithful — who confirms his brethren in the faith — he proclaims by a definitive act a doctrine pertaining to faith or morals.... The infallibility promised to the Church is also present in the body of bishops when, together with Peter's successor, they exercise the supreme Magisterium" (*Dogmatic Constitution on the Church,* 25). An infallible teaching is an exercise of the Church's extraordinary Magisterium. When a doctrine pertaining to faith and morals is proclaimed infallibly, it "must be adhered to with the obedience of faith" (*Dogmatic Constitution on the Church*, 25).

13. Is all the Church's teaching infallible?

In his infinite wisdom, God preserves the bishops, teaching in communion with the Pope, and the Pope himself from error when they propose a teaching that leads to a better understanding of Revelation in matters of faith and morals — even though they have not arrived at an infallible definition and have not proclaimed the teaching in a definitive manner. A non-infallible teaching is an exercise of the Church's ordinary Magisterium. "To this ordinary teaching the faithful 'are to adhere to it with religious assent' (*LG* 25) which, though distinct from the assent of faith, is nonetheless an extension of it" (CCC 892).

14. What is the Magisterium of the Church?

The Magisterium is the teaching office of the Church. The Pope and the bishops in communion with him are the authentic teachers endowed with the authority of Christ. They constitute the teaching office of the Church. "The mission of the Magisterium is linked to the definitive nature of the covenant established by God with his people in Christ. It is this Magisterium's task to preserve God's people from deviations and defections and to guarantee them the objective possibility of professing the true faith without error. Thus, the pastoral duty of the Magisterium is aimed at seeing to it that the People of God abides in the truth that liberates. To fulfill this service, Christ endowed the Church's shepherds with the charism of infallibility in matters of faith and morals" (CCC 890).

The Magisterium ensures the Church's fidelity to the teachings of Christ in matters of faith and morals. When the Pope and the bishops in communion with him definitively proclaim a doctrine to be infallible, they are exercising the extraordinary Magisterium of the Church. When the Pope and bishops teach authoritatively, but not infallibly, they are exercising the ordinary Magisterium of the Church. "The *ordinary* and universal *Magisterium* of the Pope and the bishops in communion with him teach the faithful the truth to believe, the charity to practice, the beatitude to hope for" (CCC 2034). In light of their responsibility to bear authoritative witness to the Word of God, the Pope and bishops teach truly and securely what Jesus wants us to believe and do.

15. Do the teachings of the Church change?

The basic teachings of the Church do not change. While the Church does not substitute new doctrines for old ones in any sense, the Church teaches and believes a living faith. The Church hands on Tradition consistently and intelligibly. In every age and culture, the Church, under the guidance of the Holy Spirit, leads us into a fuller understanding and clearer expression of God's Word. Thus, the Church might change the specific wording of her teachings to bring about a better understanding in a particular age, but the Church nevertheless hands on the same basic teachings.

16. Who are the laity?

The laity are the faithful who are incorporated into Christ by Baptism and integrated into the People of God, the Church. They "are made sharers in their particular way in the priestly, prophetic and kingly office of Christ, and have their own part to play in the mission of the whole Christian people in the Church and in the world" (*Dogmatic Constitution on the Church*, 31). The vocation of the lay faithful is to bring the Gospel of Christ especially to the social, political, and economic spheres of life. Because God has entrusted the apostolate to them, lay Christians have the responsibility to ensure that the message of salvation is made known and accepted throughout the earth. In some situations, members of the laity are the only ones who can ensure that the Good News of the coming of the Kingdom is heard and so bring others to the knowledge of Christ. "Their activity in ecclesial communities is so necessary that, for the most part, the apostolate of the pastors cannot be fully effective without it" (cf. *LG* 33) (CCC 900).

17. *What does it mean to share in the "priestly, prophetic and kingly office of Christ"?*

By virtue of their Baptism and Confirmation, the laity share in the priesthood of Jesus Christ as members of the common priesthood of the faithful. Thus, they "fulfill the call to holiness addressed to all the baptized" (CCC 941). Lay people share in the prophetic office of Christ by being his faithful witnesses in the world. "By virtue of their kingly mission, lay people have the power to uproot the rule of sin within themselves and in the world, by their self-denial and holiness of life" (cf. *LG* 36) (CCC 943).

18. *How is the Church related to the Kingdom of God and to the world?*

The Church is that part of the world that confesses Jesus as Lord. There are many in the world who do not so believe. Therefore, the Church is not identical to the world. The Kingdom of God is present where God rules his people with love and mercy. The Kingdom of God will reach its fullness only in eternity. The Church is a visible sign and instrument of the Kingdom of God on earth. Therefore, the Church and the Kingdom are closely related but not identical. The Kingdom of God and the world are not identical because part of the world is still dominated by evil and, therefore, is not included in the Kingdom of God. At the end of time, God will bring all things to completion according to his loving plan of goodness.

19. *What is the mission of the Church?*

The mission of the Church has her origin in the mission of the Son and the Holy Spirit. The mission of the Church is to proclaim the Good News of Jesus Christ to the ends of the earth, to announce the coming of the Kingdom, to be a sign of its presence in time and space, and to extend the love and mercy of God to all people. "The ultimate purpose of mission is none other than to make men share in the communion between the Father and the Son in their Spirit of love" (cf. John Paul II, *Rmiss* 23) (CCC 850).

20. *What is ecumenism?*

Christ founded one Church and bestowed on her the gift of unity from the very beginning. Through the centuries, however, large communities became separated from full communion with the Catholic Church. These ruptures have wounded the Body of Christ and caused serious divisions. Ecumenism is the promotion of unity among all Christians. It is an attitude of openness toward Christians of different denominations that seeks to learn from them, to deepen one's commitment to the Gospel of Jesus Christ, and to bring about reconciliation. "The desire to recover the unity of all Christians is a gift of Christ and a call of the Holy Spirit" (cf. *UR* 1) (CCC 820).

21. *What about non-Christian people?*

Jewish people have always had a special bond with Christians because Christianity developed from Judaism. They are the covenant people who, like Christians, are called to the Kingdom of God. Muslims acknowledge the Creator and look to Abraham as a model of faith and, as such, also have a special relationship with Christians. Buddhists, Hindus, Taoists, Shintos, and others demonstrate the wide variety of responses to the call of faith. These non-Christian religions have valid insights and valuable traditions, and they hold respectable positions in the history of the world's religions. Christianity is best served by an open dialogue among all religions.

22. *What are the "marks" of the Church?*

The "marks" of the Church are signs of her identity as a unique reality in the world. The Church is *one*. She "acknowledges one Lord, confesses one faith, is born of one Baptism, forms only one

Body, is given life by the one Spirit, for the sake of one hope (cf. Eph 4:3-5), at whose fulfillment all divisions will be overcome" (CCC 866). The Church is *holy*. "The Most Holy God is her author; Christ, her bridegroom, gave himself up to make her holy; the Spirit of holiness gives her life" (CCC 867). The Church is *catholic*. "She proclaims the fullness of the faith. She bears in herself and administers the totality of the means of salvation. She is sent out to all peoples" (CCC 868). The Church is *apostolic*. She is built on the foundation of the apostles. "She is indestructible (cf. Mt 16:18). She is upheld infallibly in the truth: Christ governs her through Peter and the other apostles, who are present in their successors, the Pope and the college of bishops" (CCC 869).

QUESTIONS FOR GROUP DISCUSSION

1. How did the Church begin?
2. In what sense is the Church the "People of God"?
3. How did the Church grow?
4. In what sense is the Church an "institution"?
5. In what sense is the Church "prophetic"?

QUESTIONS FOR PERSONAL REFLECTION

1. Do I perceive my local parish community as the "People of God"?
2. Do I need the support and encouragement of others on my journey in faith?
3. Do I see the Church as the visible sign of the Kingdom of God?
4. Do I look to the Eucharist as the bond that unites the believers around the Church's mission to proclaim the Gospel?
5. Do I recognize the need for authority in the Church?

PRAYERS OF INTERCESSION

For the Church

Let us pray, dear friends, for the holy Church of God throughout the world, that God the almighty Father guide it and gather it together so that we may worship him in peace and tranquility.

Silent prayer.

Almighty and eternal God, you have shown your glory to all nations in Christ your Son. Guide the work of your Church. Help it to persevere in faith, proclaim your name, and bring salvation to people everywhere. We ask this through Christ our Lord. Amen.

For the Pope

Let us pray for our Holy Father, Pope N., that God who chose him to be bishop may give him health and strength to guide and govern God's holy people.

Silent prayer.

Almighty and eternal God, you guide all things by your word, you govern all Christian people. In your love protect the Pope you have chosen for us. Under his leadership deepen our faith and make us better Christians. We ask this through Christ our Lord. Amen.

For the clergy and laity of the Church

Let us pray for N., our bishop, for all bishops, priests, and deacons; for all who have a special ministry in the Church and for all God's people.

Silent prayer.

Almighty and eternal God, your Spirit guides the Church and makes it holy. Listen to our prayers and help each of us in his own vocation to do your work more faithfully. We ask this through Christ our Lord. Amen.

For the unity of Christians

Let us pray for all our brothers and sisters who share our faith in Jesus Christ, that God may gather and keep together in one Church all those who seek the truth with sincerity.

Silent prayer.

Almighty and eternal God, you keep together all those you have united. Look kindly on all who follow Jesus your Son. We are all consecrated to you by our common baptism. Make us one in the fullness of faith, and keep us one in the fellowship of love. We ask this through Christ our Lord. Amen.

For the Jewish people

Let us pray for the Jewish people, the first to hear the word of God, that they may continue to grow in the love of his name and in faithfulness to his covenant.

Silent prayer.

Almighty and eternal God, long ago you gave your promise to Abraham and his posterity. Listen to your Church as we pray that the people you first made your own may arrive at the fullness of redemption. We ask this through Christ our Lord. Amen.

For those who do not believe in Christ

Let us pray for those who do not believe in Christ, that the light of the Holy Spirit may show them the way to salvation.

Silent prayer.

Almighty and eternal God, enable those who do not acknowledge Christ to find the truth as they walk before you in sincerity of heart. Help us to grow in love for one another, to grasp more fully the mystery of your godhead, and to become more perfect witnesses of your love in the sight of men. We ask this through Christ our Lord. Amen.

For those who do not believe in God

Let us pray for those who do not believe in God, that they may find him by sincerely following all that is right.

Silent prayer.

Almighty and eternal God, you created mankind so that all might long to find you and have peace when you are found. Grant that, in spite of the hurtful things that stand in their way, they may all recognize in the lives of Christians the tokens of your love and mercy, and gladly acknowledge you as the one true God and Father of us all. We ask this through Christ our Lord. Amen.

FROM THE GENERAL INTERCESSIONS OF
THE CELEBRATION OF THE LORD'S PASSION

CHAPTER 8

Mary

———

SCRIPTURE REFLECTION

And Mary said:
"My soul proclaims the greatness of the Lord;
 my spirit rejoices in God my savior.
For he has looked upon his handmaid's lowliness;
 behold, from now on will all ages call me blessed.
The Mighty One has done great things for me,
 and holy is his name.
His mercy is from age to age
 to those who fear him.
He has shown might with his arm,
 dispersed the arrogant of mind and heart.
He has thrown down the rulers from their thrones
 but lifted up the lowly.
The hungry he has filled with good things;
 the rich he has sent away empty.
He has helped Israel his servant,
 remembering his mercy,
according to his promise to our fathers,
 to Abraham and to his descendants forever."

LUKE 1:46-55

INTRODUCTION

For many, Mary is a way to reach out to a God who may at times seem distant. As the mother of Jesus Christ, she is intimately connected to God and yet is fully human. Her life demonstrates her complete dependence upon God and the absolute surrender of her will to God's. In Luke's beautiful account of the angel's announcement of Mary's pregnancy she says, "I am the handmaid of the Lord. May it be done to me according to your word" (Lk 1:38). And again in the Acts of the Apostles, Luke places her in an important position as the principal witness among the disciples awaiting the coming of the Spirit on Pentecost.

She is indeed an appropriate model for all Christians, men and women, because of her powerful and radical openness to the will of God in her life. Mary is so honored in the history of the Church precisely because of her unique relationship to Jesus. We know that Jesus is the way to the Father, but Mary's special place in salvation history makes her a powerful intercessor with God on behalf of his people.

STUDY QUESTIONS

1. *Who is Mary?*

Mary, a first-century Jewish woman, lived in Nazareth. From all eternity she was chosen by God to be the virgin mother of his only Son, Jesus, through the power of the Holy Spirit. Because she is truly the human mother of the second person of the Holy Trinity and our Redeemer, Mary is rightly called the "Mother of God" and so honored by the Church. "Mary's role in the Church is inseparable from her union with Christ and flows directly from it" (CCC 964). Thus, she is also rightly called "Mother of the Church" and honored as the preeminent model for the Church.

2. *What does Sacred Scripture tell us about Mary?*

Throughout the Old Testament the holy women prepared for the mission of Mary. Different aspects of Mary's role in salvation are found in Eve, Sarah, Hannah, Deborah, Ruth, Judith, Esther, and many other women of the Old Testament. For example, Mary is often called "the new Eve" since she is the mother of all under the new covenant inaugurated in her Son, Jesus Christ.

The New Testament records that the Virgin Mary is the human mother of the Son of God, that she was full of grace and so submitted to God's intention for her, that she was absolutely faithful to his will for her, and that her commitment to serve him was single-minded. The events of Mary's life, such as the angel's announcement that she would be the mother of God by the power of the Holy Spirit, her visit to her cousin Elizabeth, the birth of Jesus, the Holy Family's flight into Egypt to escape Herod's persecution, and her presentation of Jesus in the Temple are all very significant events in the Gospels. In particular, St. Luke's Gospel and his Acts of the Apostles present the most complete portrait of Mary. St. Matthew's Gospel stresses Mary's role as the bearer of Jesus, the long-awaited Messiah. St. John's Gospel places Mary at the wedding feast of Cana, the beginning of Jesus' public life, and at the foot of the cross on which her Son died for the salvation of the world.

3. *What did the early Church believe about Mary?*
In the first few centuries, the Church held and taught what the New Testament recorded about Mary — namely, that she was a virgin and that she was the mother of Jesus Christ, the only Son of God, through the power of the Holy Spirit. These beliefs are found in the earliest creeds of the infant Church. "From the first formulations of her faith, the Church has confessed that Jesus was conceived solely by the power of the Holy Spirit in the womb of the Virgin Mary" (CCC 496). As the Church developed, some began to deny that Jesus was really a man and that he was truly born of Mary. The Church consistently upheld both the divinity and the humanity of Jesus Christ and the virginal motherhood of Mary. "What the

Catholic faith believes about Mary is based on what it believes about Christ, and what it teaches about Mary illumines in turn its faith in Christ" (CCC 487).

4. *How could Mary give birth to a child and yet remain a virgin?*

Mary's Son, Jesus Christ, had no human father; rather, the action of God the Father through the power of the Holy Spirit was responsible for the virginal conception of Jesus. "The gospel accounts understand the virginal conception of Jesus as a divine work that surpasses all human understanding and possibility" (cf. Mt 1:18-25; Lk 1:26-38) (CCC 497). In addition the Church teaches that Mary gave birth as a virgin and remained a virgin throughout her lifetime. "The deepening of faith in the virginal motherhood led the Church to confess Mary's real and perpetual virginity even in the act of giving birth to the Son of God made man" (cf. DS 291; 294; 427; 442; 503; 571; 1880) (CCC 499).

5. *How, then, is the Virgin Mary the Mother of God?*

Mary really conceived Jesus in her womb through the power of the Holy Spirit and really gave birth to him. "Mary is truly the 'Mother of God' since she is the mother of the eternal Son of God made man, who is God himself" (CCC 509).

6. *What is the Immaculate Conception?*

God prepared Mary to be the mother of his only divine Son from all eternity. This was acknowledged by the angel Gabriel when he announced that she was "full of grace" and was to become the mother of the long-awaited Messiah. "She was, by sheer grace, conceived without sin as the most humble of creatures, the most capable of welcoming the inexpressible gift of the Almighty" (CCC 722). Mary's was an entirely unique holiness, a singular grace and privilege given her by God. She was redeemed from the moment of her conception in the womb of her mother. In 1854, Pope Pius IX formally and infallibly defined for the whole Church that, from the first moment of her life, by the grace of God, Mary was kept free from sin because she was to bear Christ the Redeemer into the world. Mary was preserved from original sin because of her unique role in salvation history. "By the grace of God Mary remained free of every personal sin her whole life long" (CCC 493).

7. What is the Assumption?

The doctrine of the Assumption, formally and infallibly defined in 1950 by Pope Pius XII, states that at the end of her life on earth, Mary was taken up to heaven, body and soul. This means that Mary was preserved from the corruption of death at the end of her life, just as she was preserved from the corruption of sin at the beginning of her life. Mary, through her assumption, provides hope for all Christians, hope that is rooted deeper still in the Resurrection of the Lord. "The Assumption of the Blessed Virgin is a singular participation in her Son's Resurrection and an anticipation of the resurrection of other Christians" (CCC 966).

8. How is the Virgin Mary the model of the Church?

Mary is the model of the Church through her absolute unconditional compliance to God's will for her, her unreserved dependence on his Son's work of redemption for her, and her absolute acceptance of the Spirit's every intention for her. In Mary we recognize the exemplary realization of the Church. "Mary goes before us all in the holiness that is the Church's mystery as 'the bride without spot or wrinkle' (Eph 5:27)" (CCC 773). She is already experiencing what the Church, still on her pilgrimage of faith, hopes for. The Second Vatican Council teaches, "In the meantime the Mother of Jesus, in the glory which she possesses in body and soul in heaven, is the image and beginning of the Church as it is to be perfected in the world to come. Likewise she shines forth on earth, until the day of the Lord shall come, a sign of certain hope and comfort to the pilgrim People of God" (*Dogmatic Constitution on the Church*, 68).

9. *Do all Christians revere the Virgin Mary as the Mother of God?*

It is recorded in Luke's Gospel that Elizabeth, Mary's cousin, greeted her as "the mother of my Lord" (Lk 1:43). Some Christians over the years, however, heard in the use of the title "Mother of God" a divine claim being made for Mary herself that they thought inappropriate. Mary is not a divine person. Her role is to bear the divine Son of God into the world, not to accede to divinity herself. When understood in her proper place in salvation history, Mary is the model of faith, humility, obedience, and trust for every Christian. "Mary, the all-holy ever-virgin Mother of God, is the masterwork of the mission of the Son and the Spirit in the fullness of time. For the first time in the plan of salvation and because his Spirit had prepared her, the Father found the *dwelling place* where his Son and his Spirit could dwell among men" (CCC 721).

10. *Is the Virgin Mary our spiritual mother?*

Mary is our spiritual mother because she is "full of grace." She was grasped by God's love so completely that she is a model of fidelity, obedience, holiness, justice, and hope. She cooperated in a unique way in Jesus' saving action. She was intimately united with the suffering of Jesus through which we are saved. "Jesus is Mary's only son, but her spiritual motherhood extends to all men whom indeed he came to save" (CCC 501). Thus, her concern includes all those for whom her Son suffered, died, and rose.

11. *Why is the Virgin Mary an object of devotion?*

The Virgin Mary is an object of devotion because she is "full of grace"; she was conceived without sin; she is the virgin Mother of Christ; she was assumed body and soul into heaven; she is the Mother and model of the Church; and she continues to intercede on behalf of the Church. The Second Vatican Council teaches that the Church rightly honors "the Blessed Virgin with special devotion. From the most ancient times the Blessed Virgin has been honored with the title of 'Mother of God,' to whose protection the faithful fly in all their dangers and needs.... This very special devotion ... differs essentially from the adoration which is given to the incarnate Word and equally to the Father and the Holy Spirit, and greatly fosters this adoration" (*Dogmatic Constitution on the Church*, 66). The Church has always encouraged devotion to Mary. Devotion to Mary, however, is not adoration. Adoration is for God alone.

12. *What are some examples of devotion to the Virgin Mary?*

Marian feasts, prayers, novenas, and pilgrimages in honor of Mary have a fitting place in the life of the Church. They should always lead the faithful to Christ, who was the center of Mary's own life from beginning to end. There are several liturgical feasts dedicated to the Blessed Mother, such as the feasts of the Immaculate Conception and the Assumption. There are many examples of Marian prayer, such as the Rosary, the Magnificat, the Angelus, the Litany of the Blessed Virgin, and the act of consecration to the Immaculate Heart of Mary. There are numerous expressions of Marian devotion that are reflective of all the various cultures in which the Gospel has taken root, such as pilgrimages to Marian shrines, veneration of Marian images, and prayers inspired by the apparitions of Our Lady in various places throughout the world.

13. *Were there really apparitions of the Virgin Mary?*

"Throughout the ages, there have been so-called 'private' revelations, some of which have been recognized by the authority of the Church. They do not belong, however, to the deposit of faith. It is not their role to improve or complete Christ's definitive Revelation, but to help live more fully by it in a certain period of history" (CCC 67). These private revelations, or appearances, such as those at Guadalupe, Lourdes, and Fátima, can be valuable reminders of Mary's unique role in salvation history. The Church has given official recognition to only a small number of the reported apparitions.

Whether the appearances actually happened is a matter for careful investigation and discernment.

14. *What are some of the apparitions of Mary that have been reported?*

In 1531, St. Juan Diego, an Aztec Indian, saw an apparition of Mary at Tepeyac hill outside Guadalupe in Mexico. She appeared as a woman of mixed blood and spoke in Juan's native language. As proof of the apparition, she told him to gather the roses that had grown out of season on the hillside and bring them to the bishop. When Juan opened his cloak at the bishop's house, the roses poured onto the floor, and the image of Mary was imprinted inside the cloak.

In 1830, St. Catherine Labouré had a vision of Mary, standing on a globe, with rays of light extending from her hands downward toward the earth. Encircling the vision were the words "O Mary, conceived without sin, pray for us who have recourse to thee."

In 1846, a young boy and girl saw a vision of Mary at LaSalette in the French Alps. Mary appeared seated on a rock with her hands covering her tears. After much dispute, a shrine was erected, and the Missionaries of LaSalette was founded.

In 1858, St. Bernadette Soubirous, a simple teenager, saw apparitions of Mary several times at Lourdes, France. Mary identified herself as the Immaculate Conception. Bernadette was told to scrape the ground nearby and drink the water from a fountain that would spring up on the site. A church was built there that attracts pilgrims seeking physical cures in the spring water.

In 1917, Mary appeared to three young children while they were tending sheep in Fátima, Portugal. In this apparition Mary revealed herself as the Lady of the Rosary and urged all to pray the Rosary for peace. A shrine was later built on the site.

QUESTIONS FOR GROUP DISCUSSION

1. Did Mary freely consent to be the Mother of God?

2. How do the Gospels portray Mary's relationship with Jesus?

3. What is the significance of Mary's virginity?

4. In what sense is the Virgin Mary "first among Christians"?

5. Is it possible to overemphasize the role of the Virgin Mary in salvation history?

QUESTIONS FOR PERSONAL REFLECTION

1. Does the Virgin Mary's absolute dependence on God make sense to me in a world where so much emphasis is placed on independence?

2. Like Mary, can I surrender my own will to the will of the Father?

3. Can I see in Mary's faith a model for my own personal growth in faith?

4. Would God's grace be more active in me if I permitted it?

SALVE REGINA

All: *Hail, Holy Queen, Mother of Mercy; our life, our sweetness, and our hope. To you do we cry, poor banished children of Eve; to you do we send up our sighs, mourning and weeping in this valley of tears. Turn then, most gracious advocate, your eyes of mercy toward us; and after this, our exile, show unto us the blessed fruit of your womb, Jesus. O clement, O loving, O sweet virgin Mary.*

Leader: *Pray for us, O holy Mother of God.*

All: *That we may be made worthy of the promises of Christ.*

Leader: *Let us pray. Almighty, everlasting God, who, by the cooperation of the Holy Spirit, did prepare the body and soul of the glorious virgin Mother, Mary, to become the fit habitation of your Son: grant that, as we rejoice in her commemoration, we may, by her loving intercession, be delivered from present evils and from everlasting death. Through the same Christ our Lord.*

All: *Amen.*

CHAPTER 9

The Future

———

SCRIPTURE REFLECTION

"What eye has not seen, and ear has not heard,
and what has not entered the human heart,
what God has prepared for those who love him."

1 CORINTHIANS 2:9

INTRODUCTION

Death is a very real part of life for each of us. Its unavoidable eventuality causes many people to dread its approach with fear and anxiety. Artists, writers, philosophers, and religious thinkers throughout history have tried to sort out and express some of the aspects of the mystery of death. For the Christian, however, the resurrection of Jesus demonstrates that the power of God alone has dominion over death. St. Paul tells us, "Christ has been raised from the dead, the firstfruits of those who have fallen asleep" (1 Cor 15:20).

Faith in the resurrection of the Lord gives rise to a prudent hope that we too will be raised by the power of the Father. In fact, that abiding hope goes beyond the merely personal to include the firm expectation that the Kingdom of God will dominate the entire created order, obliterating sin, death, and suffering for all eternity. The book of Revelation describes the situation in these words:

I heard a loud voice from the throne saying, "Behold, God's dwelling is with the human race. He will dwell with them and they will be his people and God himself will always be with them [as their God]. He will wipe every tear from their eyes, and there shall be no more death or mourning, wailing or pain, [for] the old order has passed away" [Rv 21:3-4].

STUDY QUESTIONS

1. *What is the destiny of the human race?*

   The destiny of the human race is communion with the life of the Holy Trinity, the full realization of the Kingdom of God. "At the end of time, the Kingdom of God will come in its fullness. Then the just will reign with Christ for ever, glorified in body and soul, and the material universe itself will be transformed. God will then be 'all in all' (1 Cor 15:28), in eternal life" (CCC 1060).

2. *What is the Kingdom of God?*

   God wills all people to share his life. To carry out that will, Christ inaugurated the Kingdom of God on earth. The Kingdom of God is his reign over sin, suffering, and death. It is "righteousness, peace, and joy in the holy Spirit" (Rom 14:17). The Kingdom of God is present in Christ; it is announced in the Gospel; it is anticipated especially in the Eucharist. Christ sent his disciples into the world to proclaim the coming of the Kingdom to the ends of the earth. The Church is the seed and beginning of the Kingdom of God on earth. She constantly prays for the coming of the Kingdom when Christ will hand over all creation to his Father. "At the end of time, the Kingdom of God will come in its fullness" (CCC 1042).

KNOW, LOVE, AND LIVE THE CATHOLIC FAITH

3. *What did Jesus mean when he proclaimed that the Kingdom of God was at hand?*

Jesus startled his world when he preached that the Kingdom of God was already among the people. Victory over evil, freedom from sin, and triumph over death were inaugurated in the life of Christ, and so a new age was dawning in him then and continues to free us from the bondage of evil and to reconcile us to the Father today. "The Kingdom of God lies ahead of us. It is brought near in the Word incarnate, it is proclaimed throughout the whole Gospel, and it has come in Christ's death and Resurrection. The Kingdom of God has been coming since the Last Supper and, in the Eucharist, it is in our midst. The kingdom will come in glory when Christ hands it over to his Father" (CCC 2816).

4. *Is the Kingdom of God the same as heaven?*

Heaven is the fullness of communion with the Holy Trinity. The Kingdom of God, however, has already begun to be realized here on earth in the life of the Church, the Body of Christ. It will be the definitive realization of God's plan to bring all creation into communion with him. The Kingdom of God will transform humanity and the world into "new heavens and a new earth" (2 Pt 3:13).

5. *Is the Kingdom of God the same as personal salvation?*

The Kingdom of God goes far beyond one's personal salvation to encompass the whole of creation. God's plan is to bring all things in heaven and on earth into unity in Christ. This is the Kingdom of God. "In this new universe, the heavenly Jerusalem, God will have his dwelling among men" (cf. Rev 21:5) (CCC 1044). The Kingdom of God embraces the whole of humanity, and it is not simply a private matter.

6. *Is the Kingdom of God the same as the immortality of the soul?*

The Kingdom of God goes beyond the distinction of body and soul. The coming of the Kingdom marks the transformation of all humanity and the world. It ushers the whole person into a new age. "After the universal judgment, the righteous will reign for ever with Christ, glorified in body and soul" (CCC 1042).

7. *What, then, are "heaven," "personal salvation," and the "immortality of the soul"?*

These are ways of referring to our glorious future: the fullness of life after death. They are good examples of finite descriptions of infinite reality. The Kingdom of God is the future destiny of human history, but we simply do not know precisely what this new life will be or exactly when it will be fully realized. "We know neither the moment of the consummation of the earth and of man, nor the way in which the universe will be transformed. The form of this world, distorted by sin, is passing away, and we are taught that God is preparing a new dwelling and a new earth in which righteousness dwells, in which happiness will fill and surpass all the desires of peace arising in the hearts of men" (*Pastoral Constitution on the Church in the Modern World*, 39).

8. *Is the Kingdom of God eternal life?*

Eternal life can be understood as a partial description of the Kingdom of God because it implies that what has already begun, our life, is projected in some way into a future that is not limited by evil or space or time. Eternal life is unending existence with God in the everlasting happiness of heaven for those who die in his grace and friendship. "Christ is the Lord of eternal life. Full right to pass definitive judgment on the works and hearts of men belongs to him as redeemer of the world" (CCC 679).

9. Does belief in eternal life affect how I live?

Christians who are firmly convinced that a new age is inaugurated in Christ believe God's promise of a glorious future. They believe that life is a gracious gift of God, punctuated with pain and suffering and disappointment but ultimately worthy of a special destiny. Christians experience their own limitations and ultimately their own death and yet hold to the determined belief and prudent hope that God will be victorious in them. The critical decisions of life would be quite different if all we had to look forward to was a graveyard. "By living with the mind of Christ, Christians *hasten the coming of the Reign of God*, 'a kingdom of justice, love, and peace' (*Roman Missal*, Preface of Christ the King). They do not, for all that, abandon their earthly tasks; faithful to their master, they fulfill them with uprightness, patience, and love" (CCC 2046).

10. What will eternal life with God be like?

No one knows in exact detail. But it will be a life of interpersonal love like the communion of love shared among the persons of the Holy Trinity. "This mystery of blessed communion with God and all who are in Christ is beyond all understanding and description. Scripture speaks of it in images: life, light, peace, wedding feast, wine of the kingdom, the Father's house, the heavenly Jerusalem, paradise: 'no eye has seen, nor ear heard, nor the heart of man conceived, what God has prepared for those who love him' (1 Cor 2:9)" (CCC 1027).

11. What about my personal judgment after my death?

Life provides each person the opportunity either to accept or reject God's grace. Every person will be judged immediately after death based on the person's faith and works. This is the particular judgment of one's final destiny. "Every man receives his eternal recompense in his immortal soul from the moment of his death in a particular judgment by Christ, the judge of the living and the dead"

(CCC 1051). This judgment refers the person's life to Christ and results in the person's immediate entrance into heaven, entrance into heaven after a period of purification, or immediate and everlasting damnation.

12. What is heaven?

Heaven is the perfect happiness that comes from sharing in God's divine life. "This perfect life with the Most Holy Trinity — this communion of life and love with the Trinity, with the Virgin Mary, the angels and all the blessed — is called 'heaven.' Heaven is the ultimate end and fulfillment of the deepest human longings, the state of supreme, definitive happiness" (CCC 1024). Heaven is seeing God face-to-face, "as he is" (1 Jn 3:2).

13. What is purgatory?

"Those who die in God's grace and friendship imperfectly purified, although they are assured of their eternal salvation, undergo a purification after death, so as to achieve the holiness necessary to enter the joy of God" (CCC 1054). This period of purification is called "purgatory." Sacred Scripture speaks of a "cleansing fire," which is entirely different from the eternal punishment of the damned. From the earliest time the Church has offered prayers, especially the Eucharistic sacrifice, for the dead so that they may be purified and live with God forever.

14. What is hell?

"To die in mortal sin without repenting and accepting God's merciful love means remaining separated from him for ever by our own free choice. This state of definitive self-exclusion from communion with God and the blessed is called 'hell'" (CCC 1033). It is the experience of final alienation and estrangement from God, isolation and separation from all that is good. It is the experience of eternal punishment for grave and persistent sin. God does not predestine anyone to go to hell. He does not punish sinners by sending them to hell; rather he yields to the freedom of those who choose deliberately to reject his will for their own salvation in Christ.

15. *What is the Last Judgment?*

In the final judgment, Christ vindicates God's justice and mercy. This judgment of God reveals our own involvement in sin and our need for redemption. The final judgment of God over the whole world and humanity inaugurates the final stage of God's Kingdom. Through this general judgment, all things will be brought to completion.

"The Last Judgment will come when Christ returns in glory. Only the Father knows the day and the hour; only he determines the moment of its coming. Then through his Son Jesus Christ he will pronounce the final word on all history. We shall know the ultimate meaning of the whole work of creation and of the entire economy of salvation and understand the marvellous ways by which his Providence led everything towards its final end. The Last Judgment will reveal that God's justice triumphs over all the injustices committed by his creatures and that God's love is stronger than death (cf. Song 8:6)" (CCC 1040).

16. *What is the resurrection of the body?*

The resurrection of the body refers to the resurrection of the individual whole person at the end of time when all the faithful will be raised. "By death the soul is separated from the body, but in the resurrection God will give incorruptible life to our body, transformed by reunion with our soul" (CCC 1016). The doctrine of the resurrection of the body highlights the importance of our "bodiliness" and, therefore, our solidarity with the whole human race. We hope not only for the salvation of our soul, but of our whole body. In the Kingdom of God, we are called to be fully alive in body and in soul.

17. *What is the communion of saints?*

"The communion of saints is the Church" (CCC 946). It is the unity in Christ of all those in heaven and on earth who have been redeemed by him. It refers to a communion in holy things, such as faith, the sacraments, good works, possessions and charity. It also refers to a communion of holy persons — namely, the Church in heaven and on earth.

QUESTIONS FOR GROUP DISCUSSION

1. How should Christians face death?
2. What does "final judgment" really mean?
3. What experience does heaven describe?
4. What experience does hell describe?
5. What experience does purgatory describe?
6. Is there really an afterlife?

QUESTIONS FOR PERSONAL REFLECTION

1. How do I feel about my own death?
2. Does the way I think about my own death affect how I live my life?
3. How firmly do I believe in the afterlife?
4. What is my image of heaven?

Prayer From the Mass of Christian Burial

Father, all powerful and ever-living God,
we do well always and everywhere to give you thanks.

By your power you bring us to birth.
By your providence you rule our lives.
By your command you free us at last from sin
as we return to the dust from which we came.
Through the saving death of your Son
we rise at your word to the glory of the resurrection.

Now we join the angels and the saints
as they sing their unending hymn of praise:

Holy, holy, holy Lord, God of power and might,
heaven and earth are full of your glory.
Hosanna in the highest.
Blessed is he who comes in the name of the Lord.
Hosanna in the highest.

PREFACE OF CHRISTIAN DEATH IV

CHAPTER 10
Grace

———

SCRIPTURE REFLECTION

For those who are led by the Spirit of God are children of God. For you
did not receive a spirit of slavery to fall back into fear, but you received
a spirit of adoption, through which we cry, "*Abba*, Father!" The Spirit
itself bears witness with our spirit that we are children of God, and if
children, then heirs, heirs of God and joint heirs with Christ, if only we
suffer with him so that we may also be glorified with him.

ROMANS 8:14-17

INTRODUCTION

For the Christian, life itself is life in Christ. St. Paul describes this experience by saying that "I live, no longer I, but Christ lives in me" (Gal
2:20). The abiding presence of God's own life within us transforms the
whole meaning and direction of our lives. As a result of the presence of
the Holy Spirit in our hearts, we respond openly and freely to God's
continual offer of love. We are now sons and daughters of God, "to share
in the divine nature" (2 Pt 1:4).

Our actions demonstrate the presence of God's own life within us.
We live a "graced" life that not only reflects Christian values and builds
up the Body of Christ, but also allows the person of Jesus to be trans-
parently evident and clearly active. "You are not in the flesh; on the

contrary, you are in the spirit, if only the Spirit of God dwells in you" (Rom 8:9).

STUDY QUESTIONS

1. What is justification?

Justification is the gracious action of God that frees us from sin and enables us to accept God's justice and forgiveness. It is the definitive action of God in our lives that calls us from the slavery of sin to the freedom of new life in Christ. It is God's movement through the saving action of Jesus, by which he makes us holy and just. "Justification has been merited for us by the Passion of Christ. It is granted us through Baptism. It conforms us to the righteousness of God, who justifies us. It has for its goal the glory of God and of Christ, and the gift of eternal life. It is the most excellent work of God's mercy" (CCC 2020). Justification is the process through which God draws us to a new life that we do not merit and cannot earn.

2. What are the effects of justification?

The effects of justification are the remission of sin, sanctification, and interior renewal. "Justification establishes *cooperation between God's grace and man's freedom*. On man's part it is expressed by the assent of faith to the Word of God, which invites him to conversion, and in the cooperation of charity with the prompting of the Holy Spirit who precedes and preserves his assent" (CCC 1993).

3. What is grace?

"Grace is *favor*, the *free and undeserved help* that God gives us to respond to his call to become children of God, adoptive sons, partakers of the divine nature and of eternal life" (cf. Jn 1:12-18; 17:3; Rom 8:14-17; 2 Pet 1:3-4) (CCC 1996). "Grace is a *participation in the life of God*. It introduces us into the intimacy of Trinitarian life" (CCC 1997). Grace is the gratuitous gift of God. It is not owed to us because of our performance of good works or observance of certain laws. In fact, grace enables us to perform good works and observe the law.

4. *How does a person receive God's grace?*

God offers his grace to everyone. In his loving plan of salvation, the Holy Spirit infuses the grace of Christ into our soul to heal it of sin and to sanctify it. "The *preparation of man* for the reception of grace is already a work of grace. This latter is needed to arouse and sustain our collaboration in justification through faith, and in sanctification through charity. God brings to completion in us what he has begun" (CCC 2001).

5. *What are the effects of God's grace in us?*

A person is transformed by God's grace. Recipients of God's grace share in his divine life; they participate in the life of Christ as a member of his Body, the Church; they are adopted sons and daughters of the Father; they are destined to live in communion with the Holy Trinity forever in heaven. "Grace is first and foremost the gift of the Spirit who justifies and sanctifies us. But grace also includes the gifts that the Spirit grants us to associate us with his work, to enable us to collaborate in the salvation of others and in the growth of the Body of Christ, the Church. There are *sacramental graces,* gifts proper to the different sacraments. There are furthermore *special graces* ... at the service of charity which builds up the Church (cf. 1 Cor 12)" (CCC 2003).

6. *Can a person refuse God's offer of love?*

"God's free initiative demands *man's free response,* for God has created man in his image by conferring on him, along with freedom, the power to know him and love him. The soul only enters freely into the communion of love. God immediately touches and directly moves the heart of man. He has placed in man a longing for truth and goodness that only he can satisfy" (CCC 2002). It is the nature of the human person to accept God's favor. He has implanted a longing for his love in our hearts. We are free to refuse God's offer of grace, but in doing so we would be acting against our nature. Love is what human life naturally craves. "The divine initiative in the work of grace precedes, prepares, and elicits the free response of man. Grace responds to the deepest yearnings of human freedom, calls freedom to cooperate with it, and perfects freedom" (CCC 2022).

7. *What is sanctifying grace?*

Sanctifying grace is a share in God's own life. It is God's personal presence in our lives. It is his transforming love, which marks a distinctive relationship in which we become children of God and heirs of the Kingdom of heaven. God initiates this relationship, and it is our pleasure and our duty to respond. "Sanctifying grace is an habitual gift, a stable and supernatural disposition that perfects the soul itself to enable it to live with God, to act by his love" (CCC 2000). Sanctifying grace is the source of our sanctification.

8. *What is actual grace?*

Whereas sanctifying grace is the permanent disposition to live and act in keeping with our vocation to communion with God, actual grace "refer[s] to God's interventions, whether at the beginning of conversion or in the course of the work of sanctification" (CCC 2000). Actual grace is God's assistance to accomplish specific good actions or deeds of love. It makes us aware of God's will for us in the particular circumstances of our lives and helps us to be faithful to God's plan for us. The grace to live a responsible Christian life or to take up a ministry within the Church are examples of actual graces.

9. *What is merit?*

Merit is the reward that God gives to those who love him and by his grace perform good works. It is our right by God's grace, but it is a right won for us by the charity of Christ. God's grace alone ensures the supernatural quality of our acts and makes us worthy of obtaining his promises, especially the promise of eternal life. Whatever merit we are owed in God's justice is itself a gift of his divine goodness. "We can have merit in God's sight only because of God's free plan to associate man with the work of his grace. Merit is to be ascribed in the first place to the grace of God, and secondly to man's collaboration. Man's merit is due to God" (CCC 2025).

10. Are we predestined to eternal life or eternal death?

God wills the salvation of every person. God does not predestine certain persons for eternal damnation and then withhold his love from them. "God predestines no one to go to hell (cf. Council of Orange II [529]: DS 397; Council of Trent [1547]: 1567); for this, a willful turning away from God (a mortal sin) is necessary, and persistence in it until the end" (CCC 1037). Neither is human life a series of mechanical inevitabilities determined by God. God is not the puppeteer, and we are not the puppets. God wills to save those who freely respond to his offer of love, and he wills to condemn those who freely choose to reject his free offer of love. Predestination refers to God's will for the final destiny or goal of human life.

> He has made known to us the mystery of his will in accord with his favor that he set forth in him ... to sum up all things in Christ, in heaven and on earth.
>
> In him we were also chosen, destined in accord with the purpose of the One who accomplishes all things according to the intention of his will [Eph 1:9-11].

QUESTIONS FOR GROUP DISCUSSION

1. Does God's grace "possess" a person?

2. Does God's grace make us do things we ordinarily would not do?

3. Can I "feel" God's grace within me?

4. How do I know I have God's grace within me?

5. How does predestination relate to the personal freedom of the individual?

QUESTIONS FOR PERSONAL REFLECTION

1. How close do I feel to the Lord?

2. Do I ever hear an "inner voice" speaking to me?

3. Do I have a sense that my life is sacred because the Lord dwells within?

4. Do my actions demonstrate the presence of the Lord within? Am I compassionate? Loving? Forgiving? Merciful? Peaceful? Just?

HAIL MARY

Hail, Mary, full of grace, the Lord is with thee; blessed art thou among women, and blessed is the fruit of thy womb, Jesus.

Holy Mary, Mother of God, pray for us sinners, now and at the hour of our death. Amen.

CHAPTER 11
Man

SCRIPTURE REFLECTION

Then God said, "Let us make man in our image, after our likeness. Let them have dominion over the fish of the sea, the birds of the air, and the cattle, and over all the wild animals and all the creatures that crawl on the ground."

> God created man in his image;
> in the divine image he created him;
> male and female he created them.

GENESIS 1.26-28

INTRODUCTION

Many times throughout their lives, human beings face fundamental questions of personal identity, such as "Who am I?" and "Where am I going?" We wonder about the origin of our lives, not merely in biological terms, but in spiritual terms as well. At every stage we have a natural sense of the dignity and sanctity of life, and we search for meaning and purpose. We desire happiness, peace, and personal fulfillment while we need to love and be loved. Our destiny is to be with God, who created us "in his image" (Gn 1:27), calls us "by name" (Is 43:1), has probed us and knows us (cf. Ps 139:1), and makes his dwelling within us (cf. Jn 14:23). God loves us as if we were his beloved. His life animates our lives. "In him we live and move and have our being" (Acts 17:28).

STUDY QUESTIONS

1. Who is the origin of human life?

God created man and woman a unity of body and soul. "The human person, created in the image of God, is a being at once corporeal and spiritual" (CCC 362). Of all his creatures, human beings alone are called to share in God's own life. Human beings are neither purely spiritual nor purely material beings but whole persons, body and soul. "With his openness to truth and beauty, his sense of moral goodness, his freedom and the voice of his conscience, with his longings for the infinite and for happiness, man questions himself about God's existence. In all this he discerns signs of his spiritual soul. The soul, the 'seed of eternity we bear in ourselves, irreducible to the merely material' (*GS* 18 § 1; cf. 14 § 2), can have its origin only in God" (CCC 33).

2. How is each person an image of God?

The book of Genesis tells us that God said, "Let us make man in our image, after our likeness. Let them have dominion" (Gn 1:26). Every man and woman is an image of God because we were created out of love, and "God is love" (1 Jn 4:8). We are reflections of God because we have inherent personal dignity, intelligence, freedom, conscience, and an eternal destiny. We mirror the life of the Trinity in the social dimension of our human nature. "Being in the image of God the human individual possesses the dignity of a person, who is not just something, but someone. He is capable of self-knowledge, of self-possession and of freely giving himself and entering into communion with other persons" (CCC 357).

3. Were men and women created with equal dignity?

Man and woman have the same origin in the one God. He created them with the same nature, a unity of body and soul. He created them with equal dignity. All human beings have been redeemed by the same sacrifice of Christ, and all are called to share the same destiny: communion with God for all eternity. "Man and woman have been *created*, which is to say, *willed* by God: on the one hand, in perfect equality as human persons; on the other, in their respective beings as man and woman. 'Being man' or 'being woman' is a reality which is good and willed by God: man and woman possess an inalienable dignity which comes to them immediately from God their Creator (cf. Gen 2:7, 22)" (CCC 369).

4. What is the soul?

The soul is the spiritual principle of human life. It contains the intellect and the will, through which we can respond to God's offers of love. While the soul is intangible, it animates the flesh. While it is immaterial, it gives form to the body. Human beings are the bodies of their souls and the souls of their bodies. The soul and the body together make a single living person. "The Church teaches that every spiritual soul is created immediately by God   it is not 'produced' by the parents — and also that it is immortal: it does not perish when it separates from the body at death, and it will be reunited with the body at the final Resurrection" (cf. Pius XII, *Humani Generis*: DS 3896; Paul VI, *CPG* § 8; Lateran Council V [1513]: DS 1440) (CCC 366).

5. What does it mean "to save one's soul"?

"Called to beatitude but wounded by sin, man stands in need of salvation from God. Divine help comes to him in Christ through the law that guides him and the grace that sustains him" (CCC 1949). While it is the responsibility of all human beings to work out their salvation, Christ has already won our salvation by his sacrificial death on the cross. The salvation of a person is not merely the salvation of the person's soul, but the salvation of the whole person, a unity of body and soul.

6. *What is freedom of the will?*

God wills all people to be saved. Eternal life with God is our proper destiny. Yet God does not force his saving grace on anyone. God wills that we accept freely the gift of eternal life. If God did not give us the freedom either to receive or to refuse the divine call, we would not be able to make an authentic human response at all. Freedom of the will characterizes all human action. "Freedom is the power, rooted in reason and will, to act or not to act, to do this or that, and so to perform deliberate actions on one's own responsibility. By free will one shapes one's own life" (CCC 1731). Because he has made us free, God permits us to choose actions that he forbids, to refuse the grace he offers us, and to reject the call to eternal life.

Every human life is a journey in freedom back to God. "Man is by nature and vocation a religious being. Coming from God, going toward God, man lives a fully human life only if he freely lives by his bond with God" (CCC 44).

7. *What is the purpose of human life?*

"The desire for God is written in the human heart, because man is created by God and for God; and God never ceases to draw man to himself. Only in God will he find the truth and happiness he never stops searching for" (CCC 27). The purpose of human life is to share God's own life for all eternity. We were created precisely to live in communion with God forever. God intends us to live with him in his divine beatitude beyond the end of time and for all ages. "Of all visible creatures only man is 'able to know and love his creator' (*GS* 12 § 3). He is 'the only creature on earth that God has willed for its own sake' (*GS* 24 § 3), and he alone is called to share, by knowledge and love, in God's own life. It was for this end that he was created, and this is the fundamental reason for his dignity" (CCC 356).

8. *Are Adam and Eve the parents of the human race?*

In Hebrew, *adam* means "man" and *eve* means "life." These two names signify not only two individuals but also the two sexes, from whom all humans are descended. They both owe their origin to God. In this sense Adam and Eve were our first parents. "Adam and Eve transmitted to their descendants human nature wounded by their own first sin and hence deprived of original holiness and justice; this deprivation is called 'original sin'" (CCC 417).

9. *Is the Catholic doctrine of the creation of man and woman necessarily opposed to the scientific theory of evolution?*

God created each individual human soul from nothing. No theory of evolution can account for this act. God also created all that exists in the world of nature. This creative action could have found expression in an evolutionary process. The creation stories found in the book of Genesis are not scientific accounts and therefore are not opposed to the scientific theory of evolution, unless that theory excludes God's absolutely original creation of each individual and immortal soul. "The theory of natural evolution, understood in a sense that does not exclude divine causality, is not in principle opposed to the truth about the creation of the visible world, as presented in the Book of Genesis" (Pope John Paul II, *Catechesis on Creation*, General Audience, January 29, 1986).

10. *What is original sin?*

Original sin is the personal sin in which the first human beings freely chose to disobey God's command and follow their own will rather than God's will. By this choice, sin, suffering, and death entered the world. As a consequence of this sin, our first parents lost the original holiness and justice they had received from God, and the presence of sin became universal in the world. In addition to their personal sin, Adam and Eve transmitted original sin to their descendants. In this sense, original sin describes the fallen state of human nature, which affects every person born into the world. "As a result of original sin, human nature is weakened in its powers; subject to ignorance, suffering, and the domination of death; and inclined to sin" (CCC 418). Although the newborn child is not personally responsible for this sin, the child is nonetheless subject to its effect, a diminished capacity to love God above all else.

QUESTIONS FOR GROUP DISCUSSION

1. At what point did God create human life?
2. What is a soul?
3. Why did God create human life?
4. How do we know God loves us?
5. Is original sin something we do?
6. How can God love us if we are sinners?
7. Isn't human life less sacred if we evolved from lower forms of life?
8. In the evolutionary chain, when did animals stop and humans begin?

QUESTIONS FOR PERSONAL REFLECTION

1. Who am I?
2. Where am I going?
3. What do I value?
4. What is my purpose in life?
5. What does God have to do with my identity?

PRAYER FOR UNION WITH GOD

If, Lord, thy love for me is strong
As this which binds me unto thee,
What holds me from thee, Lord, so long,
What holds thee, Lord, so long from me?

O soul, what then desirest thou?
— Lord, I would see, who thus choose thee.
What fears can yet assail thee now?
— All that I fear is to lose thee.

Love's whole possession I entreat,
Lord, make my soul thine own abode,
And I will build a nest so sweet
It may not be too poor for God.

O soul in God hidden from sin,
What more desires for thee remain,
Save but to love, and love again,
And all on flame with love within,
Love on, and turn to love again?

ST. TERESA OF ÁVILA

PART TWO

Catholic Life

Now that you have spent some time learning and reflecting on the core content of the Catholic faith, it is important for you to know that faith is more than a system of beliefs, teachings, and doctrines. Faith is also an attitude of trust in the credibility and dependability of a loving God.

Trusting complements believing, but is distinct from it. Basically, trusting is a work of the heart; believing is a work of the mind. Trust presumes acceptance, freedom, and confidence within the context of a personal relationship between the believer and God. Trust stresses the intimate relationship in which God calls us by name and promises to be eternally faithful. This kind of trust finds expression in our loyalty, love, and attachment for the God who in Jesus no longer calls us "slaves" but "friends." It spills out of us naturally, enthusiastically, like a child's desire to be in accord with all creation.

This section is an exploration of a basic attitude or outlook that is common among many Catholics. This is not as easy to understand as the previous section on Catholic faith was. Teachings, doctrines, traditions, and tenets can be easily learned, even if they are not believed. But developing a Catholic perspective on life and on the world involves a personal decision to integrate what we believe with what we have learned and to value these closely held beliefs. If we believe what we have learned about the Catholic faith, then our approach to or our stance before life changes. That approach in the Catholic tradition is expressed in our moral and sacramental lives.

These are the fundamental themes of this section:

- **Morality** — deals with the ethical questions raised by the Ten Commandments, whether the end justifies the means, and the role of one's life situation in making moral decisions.
- **Moral Conscience** — focuses on how we know moral goodness from moral evil, how we form our conscience, and the ethical dilemmas we sometimes face.
- **Sin** — probes the questions of the nature of sin and what is required to commit a mortal sin.
- **Sacraments in General** — addresses what a sacrament is, how the sacraments originated, and the meaning of each of the sacraments.
- **Ecclesial Lay Ministry** — treats questions about the role of lay ministers in the Church, the relationship of lay and ordained ministers, and the dignity of the lay vocation.
- **The Family of the Church** — treats the many names or models of the Church, the role of religious life in the Church, and the place that saints hold in the faith life of the Church.

CHAPTER 12
Morality

―――

SCRIPTURE REFLECTION

For through the law I died to the law, that I might live for God. I have been crucified with Christ; yet I live, no longer I, but Christ lives in me; insofar as I now live in the flesh, I live by faith in the Son of God who has loved me and given himself up for me.

GALATIANS 2:19-21

INTRODUCTION

Faith is more than a positive attitude toward life and God. Faith is a commitment to action in Christ. But we often ask ourselves the questions "What does my faith have to do with how I live?" and "How do I know how to live?" Those questions need to be asked within the context of a relationship with God. That relationship is the covenant. It is God's pledge to be our God and our pledge to be his people. It has both personal and communal dimensions.

We have been called by the Father to share his own life. We have been invited to live in imitation of Christ and, if we choose to accept the Father's invitation, we are guided in living Christ's life by the abiding presence of the Holy Spirit within us. It is the Spirit who binds us to one another in a loving community, the Body of Christ, the Church. We do not attempt to imitate Christ all alone but rather within a community of support and encouragement. We live our lives "differently" because we are "in Christ." What we do in life is directly related to what we believe about life and what our belief compels us to accomplish.

STUDY QUESTIONS

1. *What is Christian life?*

   Christian life is life in Christ. Through Christ we share in God's own life, the life of grace. Therefore, Christian life is not merely a life that is animated by Christian values and strives to do good and avoid evil; rather, Christian life is an intimate participation in God's own life. "Incorporated into *Christ* by Baptism, Christians are 'dead to sin and alive to God in Christ Jesus' and so participate in the life of the Risen Lord (Rom 6:11 and cf. 6:5; cf. Col 2:12). Following Christ and united with him (cf. Jn 15:5), Christians can strive to be 'imitators of God as beloved children, and walk in love' (Eph 5:1-2) by conforming their thoughts, words and actions to the 'mind ... which is yours in Christ Jesus' (Phil 2:5), and by following his example (cf. Jn 13:12-16)" (CCC 1694).

2. *Who is the model of Christian life?*

   The model of Christian life is Jesus Christ. This does not mean that Christians are to do only what Jesus did and decide just as Jesus decided in particular situations. Jesus is the model for Christian life in a much deeper sense. "It is by looking to him in faith that Christ's faithful can hope that he himself fulfills his promises in them, and that, by loving him with the same love with which he has loved them, they may perform works in keeping with their dignity" (CCC 1698). All things were created in Christ and, as such, he is the model for that which is good. When Christians seek the good, they seek Christ. It is in this sense that Jesus is the model for Christian life.

3. Did Jesus Christ come primarily to teach a moral code?

Jesus Christ came to announce the nearness of the Kingdom of God. He was deeply rooted in the Jewish moral tradition and taught his disciples to love one another as he loved them. He taught powerfully by his words and by his life, but he did not come primarily to announce a moral code or to assist people in living good lives. He is our Redeemer, not merely a moralist. With his coming a whole new order of existence was inaugurated, not simply a new morality. He came to share God's own life with us, not merely a series of insights about how to be good. "The moral law finds its fullness and its unity in Christ. Jesus Christ is in person the way of perfection. He is the end of the law, for only he teaches and bestows the justice of God" (CCC 1953).

To see Jesus Christ as only the exemplar of a new moral code is to miss the point of his mission. He invites us to become sons and daughters of God and to respond to God's offer of love by doing his will and living morally good lives, but primarily he ushers in a whole new age. This understanding does not diminish the importance of living Christian virtues in our lives, but places Christian moral life in its proper perspective.

4. What was Jesus' moral tradition?

Jesus' moral tradition was the Torah, the Law of Moses found in the first five books of the Old Testament. The Law of Moses is intimately linked with the covenant, or loving bond between God and the people of Israel, which was established with Noah, Abraham, Moses, and David in the Old Testament and with all humanity through the blood of Christ in the New Testament. The clearest expression of the Torah ("instruction") is in the Ten Commandments, which are a unique manifestation of the covenant. While Jesus' moral teaching was based on the Mosaic instruction "to love God with all your heart, with all your soul and with all your might, and to love your neighbor as yourself," Jesus extended that teaching to mean self-giving and self-sacrifice. Jesus' moral roots are firmly in the Mosaic Law, but he offered a new standard of behavior. We are to love one another "as I have loved you."

"The perfect fulfillment of the Law could be the work of none but the divine legislator, born subject to the Law in the person of the Son (cf. Gal 4:4). In Jesus, the Law no longer appears engraved on tables of stone but 'upon the heart' of the Servant who becomes 'a covenant to the people,' because he will 'faithfully bring forth justice' (Jer 31:33; Isa 42:3, 6)"(CCC 580).

5. *What is the natural law?*

Natural law is the basic moral law that governs human life. "The natural law, present in the heart of each man and established by reason, is universal in its precepts and its authority extends to all men. It expresses the dignity of the person and determines the basis for his fundamental rights and duties" (CCC 1956). The natural law is God's plan for human life. It is the objective moral order to which our behavior ought to conform in order to achieve the fulfillment of God's plan. God has revealed the essential requirements of a good moral life in the natural law. The fundamental principles of natural law follow from our being who we are, human beings in search of goodness and truth. "The natural law is immutable, permanent throughout history. The rules that express it remain substantially valid. It is a necessary foundation for the erection of moral rules and civil law" (CCC 1979).

6. *What is the Old Law?*

"The Old Law is the first stage of revealed Law. Its moral prescriptions are summed up in the Ten Commandments. The precepts of the Decalogue lay the foundations for the vocation of man fashioned in the image of God; they prohibit what is contrary to the love of God and neighbor and prescribe what is essential to it. The Decalogue is a light offered to the conscience of every man to make God's call and ways known to him and to protect him against evil" (CCC 1962). The Old Law prepares us for conversion and faith in the Redeemer. It prepares us to receive the Gospel.

7. *What are the Ten Commandments, and what issues in Catholic life do they raise for careful consideration and informed judgment?*

"**1. I am the** LORD **your God: you shall not have strange Gods before me.**" Some of the moral issues raised by the first commandment are the proper relationship between God and man, worship of one God, use of religious articles, spiritism, and worship of things: money, power, success, self, etc.

"**2. You shall not take the name of the Lord your God in vain.**" Some of the moral issues raised by the second commandment are respect for God's person and name and for those who represent him, taking oaths, sacrilege, blasphemy, misuse of religion, and simony.

"**3. Remember to keep holy the** LORD**'s day.**" Some of the moral issues raised by the third commandment are participation in Sunday Eucharist, appropriate use of time, and communal prayer.

"**4. Honor your father and your mother.**" Some of the moral issues raised by the fourth commandment are parental authority, parental responsibility, obedience to parents, respect for parents, parental limitations, and the rights of children.

"**5. You shall not kill.**" Some of the moral issues raised by the fifth commandment are the sanctity of life; respect for life; concern for the poor, the hungry, and the oppressed; the unjust aggressor; capital punishment; abortion; euthanasia; health care; drugs; alcohol; organ transplants; allocation of scarce medical resources; sterilization; genetic engineering; cloning; pacifism; nonviolence; and just-war theory.

"6. You shall not commit adultery." Some of the moral issues raised by the sixth commandment are human sexuality, the virtue of chastity, virginity, celibacy, Christian marriage, infidelity, artificial insemination, prostitution, promiscuity, divorce, remarriage, birth control, premarital sex, masturbation, homosexuality, transvestism, obscenity, pornography, and immodesty.

"7. You shall not steal." Some of the moral issues raised by the seventh commandment are property rights, theft, larceny, embezzlement, looting, con games, non-payment of just debts, tampering with labels, false weights and measures, restitution, insurance, suits in court, legal contracts, gambling, cheating, income tax, business practices, fair pricing, copyrights and patents, bankruptcy, and the common good.

"8. You shall not bear false witness against your neighbor." Some of the moral issues raised by the eighth commandment are personal rights, defamation of character, lying, limited right to the truth, personal right to a good name, insults, rash judgment, calumny, detraction, the right to security, the right to privacy, professional secrecy, and promises.

"9. You shall not covet your neighbor's wife." The moral issues raised by the ninth commandment are much like those pertaining to the sixth commandment.

"10. You shall not covet your neighbor's goods" (CCC — from "A Traditional Catechetical Formula" in "Part Three: Life in Christ"). The moral issues raised by the tenth commandment are much like those pertaining to the seventh commandment.

8. *What is the New Law, or the moral teaching of Jesus?*

"The New Law or the Law of the Gospel is the perfection here on earth of the divine law, natural and revealed. It is the work of Christ and is expressed particularly in the Sermon on the Mount. It is also the work of the Holy Spirit and through him it becomes the interior law of charity" (CCC 1965). The whole New Law is summarized in Jesus' command to love one another as he has loved us. Thus, the New Law is called a "law of love" because it invites us to act out of love rather than fear. It is called a "law of grace" because the life of faith and the sacraments confer the grace to act in charity and justice. It is called a "law of freedom" because it sets us free from the ritual and juridical observances of the Old Law.

9. What is the Sermon on the Mount?

In the Sermon on the Mount, Christ presented the Beatitudes (Mt 5:3-11), his teachings on the meaning of true happiness and the way to achieve it. These teachings elevate and orient the directives of the Old Law toward the Kingdom of heaven. They describe the charity of Christ and the vocation of the Christian faithful. "The Lord's Sermon on the Mount, far from abolishing or devaluing the moral prescriptions of the Old Law, releases their hidden potential and has new demands arise from them: it reveals their entire divine and human truth. It does not add new external precepts, but proceeds to reform the heart, the root of human acts, where man chooses between the pure and the impure (cf. Mt 15:18-19), where faith, hope, and charity are formed and with them the other virtues" (CCC 1968).

10. What are the Beatitudes and some of the virtues they encourage?

"Blessed are the poor in spirit, for theirs is the kingdom of heaven" (dependence on God, the virtue of religion, piety).

"Blessed are those who mourn, for they shall be comforted" (hope, contrition, compassion).

"Blessed are the meek, for they shall inherit the earth" (reliance on God, trust, humility, hope).

"Blessed are those who hunger and thirst for righteousness, for they shall be satisfied" (submission to God's will, justice, righteousness). "Blessed are the merciful, for they shall obtain mercy" (forgiveness, patience, understanding, compassion). "Blessed are the pure in heart, for they shall see God" (right judgment, prudence, obedience). "Blessed are the peacemakers, for they shall be called sons of God" (reconciliation, justice). "Blessed are those who are persecuted for righteousness' sake, / for theirs is the kingdom of heaven" (piety, resignation, justice, patience) (CCC 1716).

11. *What is the function of external laws and rules?*

"Law is a rule of conduct enacted by competent authority for the sake of the common good. The moral law presupposes the rational order, established among creatures for their good and to serve their final end, by the power, wisdom, and goodness of the Creator. All law finds its first and ultimate truth in the eternal law. Law is declared and established by reason as a participation in the providence of the living God, Creator and Redeemer of all" (CCC 1951).

External laws and rules are formulations of the inner law of grace. They are the embodiment of the wisdom and tradition of the community of faith. They describe, in an external way, the internal guidance of the Holy Spirit. They are legal formulations in the visible world of human behavior that reflect the invisible grace of the Holy Spirit alive in us. We need external precepts and rules to monitor personal rationalizations and misunderstandings of the life of the Spirit within us.

12. *What constitutes a moral act?*

"The morality of human acts depends on: the object chosen; the end in view or the intention; and the circumstances of the action"

(CCC 1750). The goodness of the object, the intention, and the circumstances together constitute a morally good act. The object is the actual good result intended to be achieved by the moral act. The intention is the purpose the person has in mind in pursuing the action. The circumstances are the conditions in which the action is performed.

13. *What part do circumstances or a given situation play in making morally good or morally evil choices?*

Circumstances can alter the morality of an act, because every act is a personal act, and every person acts in circumstances. The objective moral good or moral evil of an act binds the person in general but not in all possible circumstances. For example, to kill another person is morally evil, but to kill another person in self-defense is not. However, "the *circumstances*, including the consequences, are secondary elements of a moral act. They contribute to increasing or diminishing the moral goodness or evil of human acts (for example, the amount of a theft). They can also diminish or increase the agent's responsibility (such as acting out of a fear of death). Circumstances of themselves cannot change the moral quality of acts themselves; they can make neither good nor right an action that is in itself evil" (CCC 1754).

14. *Does this mean that the end justifies the means?*

No. One may never do what is morally evil in order to achieve a good end. Sometimes, however, it is necessary to do a physical evil so that good may come out of it — for example, to cut off one's leg in order to save one's life. "There are concrete acts that it is always wrong to choose, because their choice entails a disorder of the will, i.e., a moral evil. One may not do evil so that good may result from it" (CCC 1761).

QUESTIONS FOR GROUP DISCUSSION

1. Are there objectively good and objectively evil acts?
2. How does faith in God affect our relationships with others?
3. In what sense are Christians supposed to imitate Christ?
4. What are some practical guidelines for living the Christian life?
5. What are some of the major moral issues that face us today?
6. How can we be sure that we are doing the right thing in a certain situation?

QUESTIONS FOR PERSONAL REFLECTION

1. Does my faith affect the ordinary decisions I make in my daily life?
2. Does my faith affect my relationships at home, at work, and in the community?
3. Do I think of myself as living in Christ?
4. Is my life any different than a good atheist's?

THE TWO WAYS

I

Happy those who do not follow
the counsel of the wicked,
Nor go the way of sinners,
nor sit in company with scoffers.
Rather, the law of the LORD is their joy;
God's law they study day and night.
They are like a tree
planted near streams of water,
that yields its fruit in due season;
Its leaves never wither;
whatever they do prospers.

II

But not the wicked!
They are like chaff driven by the wind.
Therefore the wicked will not survive judgment,
nor will sinners in the assembly of the just.
The LORD watches over the way of the just,
but the way of the wicked leads to ruin.

PSALM 1

CHAPTER 13
Moral Conscience

SCRIPTURE REFLECTION

So I declare and testify in the Lord that you must no longer live as the Gentiles do, in the futility of their minds; darkened in understanding, alienated from the life of God because of their ignorance, because of their hardness of heart, they have become callous and have handed themselves over to licentiousness for the practice of every kind of impurity to excess. That is not how you learned Christ, assuming that you have heard of him and were taught in him, as truth is in Jesus, that you should put away the old self of your former way of life, corrupted through deceitful desires, and be renewed in the spirit of your minds, and put on the new self, created in God's way in righteousness and holiness of truth.

EPHESIANS 4:17-24

INTRODUCTION

In developing a well-formed Christian conscience, a person needs to have a sense of right and wrong, an understanding of basic moral principles, responsibility for personal behavior, and careful attention to the teachings of the Church. In its *Declaration on Religious Freedom*, the Second Vatican Council teaches:

In the formation of their consciences, the Christian faithful ought carefully to attend to the sacred and certain doctrine of the Church. The Church is, by the will of Christ, the teacher of the truth. It is her duty to give utterance to, and authoritatively to teach, that truth which is Christ himself, and also to declare and confirm by her authority those principles of the moral order which have their origins in human nature itself [n. 14].

We are morally obligated to follow our consciences, but this does not mean that whatever way our consciences direct us will always be the correct way. In our search to conform our will to God's, we seek to carry out our responsibilities and in the process discover our dignity. Later on in the Second Vatican Council's *Pastoral Constitution on the Church in the Modern World*, we read:

In the depths of his conscience, man detects a law which he does not impose upon himself, but which holds him to obedience. Always summoning him to love good and avoid evil, the voice of conscience when necessary speaks to his heart: do this, shun that. For man has in his heart a law written by God; to obey it is the very dignity of man; according to it he will be judged. Conscience is the most secret core and sanctuary of a man. There he is alone with God, whose voice echoes in his depths [n. 16].

STUDY QUESTIONS

1. How does the Christian know what is morally good or morally evil?
The Christian knows what is morally good or morally evil by the judgment of conscience. One's moral conscience directs the person to do good and avoid evil. It makes particular judgments that either approve a good act or reject an evil one. The Holy Spirit sheds the light of the Gospel on the knowledge of good and evil in a variety of ways: the Church's tradition, her teachings, prayer, and

dialogue. Human experience, in conjunction with the light of the Gospel, assists us in putting the knowledge of good and evil in its proper, practical context and helps us to decide prudently how to act. "When he listens to his conscience, the prudent man can hear God speaking" (CCC 1777).

2. *What is conscience?*

"Conscience is a judgment of reason by which the human person recognizes the moral quality of a concrete act" (CCC 1796). It is not merely feeling or emotion. It is rooted in the depths of a person, in the person's self-understanding and awareness. "Conscience is man's most secret core, and his sanctuary. There he is alone with God whose voice echoes in his depths" (*Pastoral Constitution on the Church in the Modern World*, 16). Conscience is a person's experience of himself or herself as a moral agent, a decider about personal actions. Conscience enables one to take responsibility for the concrete acts he or she performs. Conscience includes the perception of the principles of morality, the application of those principles in specific circumstances, and the practical judgment about the good or evil of concrete acts that will be performed or that have already been performed.

3. *How do we form our conscience?*

The formation of conscience is a lifelong task. In forming a correct conscience, we are seeking to discover the good that God wills and to which the human person is drawn. The Second Vatican Council teaches in its *Declaration on Human Freedom*, "In the formation of their consciences, the Christian faithful ought carefully to attend to the sacred and certain doctrine of the Church" (n. 14). In addition, we form our conscience by acquiring whatever information will help us come to the morally good decision. The light of the Gospel, expert opinions, prayer, study, others' experience, and personal experience provide the information necessary for the formation of one's conscience. "A well-formed conscience is upright and truthful. It formulates its judgments according to reason, in conformity with the true good willed by the wisdom of the Creator. Everyone must avail himself of the means to form his conscience" (CCC 1798).

4. Can our conscience err?

The judgments of our conscience can be mistaken, even if we sincerely seek to know what is morally good. Through the loss of original holiness, human nature includes the inclination to sin. Moral conscience can remain ignorant and consequently can make erroneous judgments. "Such ignorance and errors are not always free of guilt" (CCC 1801). Each of us is responsible to form our conscience correctly. If we do not make every effort to discover what is true and good, we deserve the blame for the evil we commit or the good we fail to do. "Ignorance of Christ and his Gospel, bad example given by others, enslavement to one's passions, assertion of a mistaken notion of autonomy of conscience, rejection of the Church's authority and her teaching, lack of conversion and of charity: these can be at the source of errors of judgment in moral conduct" (CCC 1792).

5. Aren't we supposed to follow our conscience?

"A human being must always obey the certain judgment of his conscience. If he were deliberately to act against it, he would condemn himself" (CCC 1790). Since our conscience expresses our considered judgment about the moral good or evil of a particular act, we are obliged to follow it, even if — unknown to us — it is mistaken. To act against the advice of our conscience would be to do what we have judged to be wrong. We have a serious obligation, however, to ensure that our conscience is well formed by the authoritative teachings of the Church. "The Word of God is the light for our path (cf. Ps 119:105); we must assimilate it in faith and prayer and put it into practice" (CCC 1785).

6. *What if a person's decision in conscience is opposed to the official teachings of the Church?*

The truth of Christ and the teachings of the Church have the primary place in the formation of one's conscience. Catholics are obligated to listen, submit freely, and give the assent of faith to the Word of God as authentically interpreted and taught by the Church's Magisterium. The teachings of the Church represent centuries of experience across cultural and geographical divisions. The Holy Spirit has confirmed these teachings to be the truth of Christ. They are presumed to be true and authentic. In the Church, there is a legitimate pluralism that should not be confused with dissent. Such pluralism seeks diverse considerations or applications of a particular doctrine. Dissent, on the other hand, "is opposed to ecclesial communion and to a correct understanding of the hierarchical constitution of the People of God" (Pope John Paul II, *The Splendor of Truth*, 113).

QUESTIONS FOR GROUP DISCUSSION

1. What are the elements of a well-formed Christian conscience?
2. Is it possible to reform one's conscience?
3. How does a person make moral decisions and judgments?
4. How do changes in one's personality affect one's conscience?
5. How do changes in one's life situation affect one's conscience?
6. What happens if a person's conscience tells him or her to do something that the Church forbids?

QUESTIONS FOR PERSONAL REFLECTION

1. What ordinary moral decisions do I make?
2. What moral principles usually guide those decisions?
3. Do I know what the Church teaches on the major moral questions of our time?
4. Am I open to reforming my conscience when necessary?

PRAYER FOR GUIDANCE

I

Out of the depths I call to you, LORD;
Lord, hear my cry!
May your ears be attentive
to my cry for mercy.
If you, LORD, mark our sins,
Lord, who can stand?
But with you is forgiveness
and so you are revered.

II

I wait with longing for the LORD,
my soul waits for his word.
My soul looks for the Lord
more than sentinels for daybreak.
More than sentinels for daybreak,
let Israel look for the LORD,
For with the LORD is kindness,
with him is full redemption,
And God will redeem Israel
from all their sins.

PSALM 130

CHAPTER 14

Sin

═══

SCRIPTURE REFLECTION

Therefore, sin must not reign over your mortal bodies so that you obey their desires. And do not present the parts of your bodies to sin as weapons for wickedness, but present yourselves to God as raised from the dead to life and the parts of your bodies to God as weapons for righteousness. For sin is not to have any power over you, since you are not under the law but under grace.

What then? Shall we sin because we are not under the law but under grace? Of course not! Do you not know that if you present yourselves to someone as obedient slaves, you are slaves of the one you obey, either of sin, which leads to death, or of obedience, which leads to righteousness? But thanks be to God that, although you were once slaves of sin, you have become obedient from the heart to the pattern of teaching to which you were entrusted.

ROMANS 6:12-17

INTRODUCTION

When we deliberately reject God's offer of his own love and his own life, we sin. Through sin we fail to love God, and we subvert his plan for us. Sin ruptures our relationships with God, others, ourselves, and the environment in which we live. Division replaces union in the life of the sinner. Discord replaces harmony. Exploitation and manipulation, rather than justice and love, become the motivating force behind human action.

In chapters 3 through 11 in the book of Genesis, the story of the fall of the human race is told. Out of pride, Adam rejects God and immediately experiences alienation from God. Adam hides himself from God but is confronted with his evil, which he tries to blame on Eve. Already the tragedy of sin has distorted human relationships. In the succeeding chapters, sin spreads out across the earth in various forms until the Great Flood washes creation clean of its destruction and subversion. The story clearly develops a side of human experience that is not very pleasant, but the fact of the presence of moral evil in the world is indisputable. For us, however, sin does not have the upper hand. Human nature is not corrupt but is indeed capable of enormous good, thanks to the redemptive love of the Father in Jesus. "God proves his love for us in that while we were still sinners Christ died for us" (Rom 5:8). It is difficult for us to imagine, but God loves us even though we are sinners.

STUDY QUESTIONS

1. What is sin?

Sin is an offense against God, a barrier to his love and the love of neighbor. It is the deliberate choice to act against God's will. It is specific action or inaction contrary to the law of God. "Sin is an offense against reason, truth, and right conscience; it is failure in genuine love for God and neighbor caused by a perverse attachment to certain goods. It wounds the nature of man and injures human solidarity" (CCC 1849).

2. What is mortal sin?

Mortal sin is the free and deliberate rejection of God. It is the conscious and free decision to do what is gravely wrong. "*Mortal sin destroys charity in the heart of man by a grave violation of God's law; it turns man away from God, who is his ultimate end and his beatitude, by preferring an inferior good to him*" (CCC 1855). In mortal sin, we separate ourselves from God's friendship and deepen our alienation from God. Mortal sin can either be a particular action or a general condition of alienation from God. Mortal sin deals a deadly blow to our relationship with God and with the Church, the People of God. If mortal sin is unredeemed by repentance and God's forgiveness, the eternal death of hell is the result. As long as it is not final, however, God's grace can effect conversion. "Where sin increased, grace overflowed all the more" (Rom 5:20).

3. What is required to commit a mortal sin?

"For a *sin* to be *mortal*, three conditions must together be met: 'Mortal sin is sin whose object is grave matter and which is also committed with full knowledge and deliberate consent' (*RP* 17 § 12)" (CCC 1857). Since mortal sin is a free choice to reject God's love, the matter under consideration must be of the most serious kind, the kind that destroys our relationship with God. In addition to serious matter, the person must judge the action to be seriously wrong and must perform the action freely and deliberately. In other words, we must use our basic human freedom to reject God who offers salvation. Serious matter and full liberty must converge in the deliberate decision to shatter severely one's relationship with God. Trivial matter, insufficient knowledge of the evil, or restricted freedom in performing the evil act does not constitute mortal sin.

4. What are grave matter, full knowledge, and deliberate consent?

Grave matter refers to serious actions that have severe consequences. Full knowledge means a thorough knowledge of the sinful character of the act and its opposition to God's law. Deliberate consent involves the carefully considered personal choice to commit the act. "To choose deliberately — that is, both knowing it and willing it — something gravely contrary to the divine law and to the ultimate end of man is to commit a mortal sin. This destroys in us the charity without which eternal beatitude is impossible" (CCC 1874).

5. What is venial sin?

Venial sin is a less serious act that is inconsistent with our basic attitude toward God. It diminishes but does not destroy God's life in us. Venial sin is a shortcoming, a lapse, a flaw in our overall pattern of goodness. It has an erosive effect on God's love in us, but not to the point of obliteration. It is a less serious offense against God's law. "One commits *venial sin* when, in a less serious matter, he does not observe the standard prescribed by the moral law, or when he disobeys the moral law in a grave matter, but without full knowledge or without complete consent" (CCC 1862).

6. What is social sin?

Social sin is the effect of personal sin over time that "[gives] rise to social situations and institutions that are contrary to divine goodness" (CCC 1869). It is the systemic creation of social structures of sin and unjust attitudes that inhibit groups or individuals from developing themselves within that society. By analogy this sin is called "social sin." However, individual persons make the decisions to create or sustain structures that suppress people. Individual persons assume basic attitudes that lead them to constrain the legitimate freedom of others. To legislate a tax system that benefits one group to the detriment of another, to legislate inequitable educational policies, to institutionalize racial discrimination, to declare an unjust war, or to deny the rights of laborers to organize would generally be considered examples of social sin. It should be noted, however, that the structures that perpetuate social injustice do not sin. The people responsible for those structures are the ones who sin.

QUESTIONS FOR GROUP DISCUSSION

1. How does sin affect one's relationship to God?
2. What is the difference between mortal sin and venial sin?
3. What are the personal consequences of sin?
4. Can we do anything about social evil?

QUESTIONS FOR PERSONAL REFLECTION

1. What is my personal involvement in sin?
2. Do I face up to the sin in my life?
3. Do I try to change the patterns of my life that are sinful?
4. Can I distinguish between mortal and venial sin?
5. How do I understand the fact that Jesus Christ died for my sins?

PRAYER FOR MERCY

I

Have mercy on me, God, in your goodness;
*   in your abundant compassion blot out my offense.*
Wash away all my guilt;
*   from my sin cleanse me.*
For I know my offense;
*   my sin is always before me.*
Against you alone have I sinned;
*   I have done such evil in your sight*
That you are just in your sentence,
*   blameless when you condemn.*
True, I was born guilty,
*   a sinner, even as my mother conceived me.*
Still, you insist on sincerity of heart;
*   in my inmost being teach me wisdom.*
Cleanse me with hyssop, that I may be pure;
*   wash me, make me whiter than snow.*
Let me hear sounds of joy and gladness;
*   let the bones you have crushed rejoice.*

II

Turn away your face from my sins;
*   blot out all my guilt.*
A clean heart create for me, God;
*   renew in me a steadfast spirit.*
Do not drive me from your presence,
*   nor take from me your holy spirit.*
Restore my joy in your salvation;
*   sustain in me a willing spirit.*

I will teach the wicked your ways,
  that sinners may return to you.
Rescue me from death, God, my saving God,
  that my tongue may praise your healing power.
Lord, open my lips;
  my mouth will proclaim your praise.
For you do not desire sacrifice;
  a burnt offering you would not accept.
My sacrifice, God, is a broken spirit;
  God, do not spurn a broken, humbled heart.

III

Make Zion prosper in your good pleasure;
  rebuild the walls of Jerusalem.
Then you will be pleased with proper sacrifice,
  burnt offerings and holocausts;
  then bullocks will be offered on your altar.

PSALM 51

CHAPTER 15
Sacraments in General

SCRIPTURE REFLECTION

Jesus answered and said to him, "Amen, amen, I say to you, no one can see the kingdom of God without being born from above." Nicodemus said to him, "How can a person once grown old be born again? Surely he cannot reenter his mother's womb and be born again, can he?" Jesus answered, "Amen, amen, I say to you, no one can enter the kingdom of God without being born of water and Spirit. What is born of flesh is flesh and what is born of spirit is spirit. Do not be amazed that I told you, 'You must be born from above.' The wind blows where it wills, and you can hear the sound it makes, but you do not know where it comes from or where it goes; so it is with everyone who is born of the Spirit."

JOHN 3:3-8

INTRODUCTION

The Catholic Church is a sacramental community — that is, a people who gather to celebrate their faith in signs and symbols. The sacraments are prayerful moments of encounter with the Lord. They are fundamental experiences of God's love, which shape the community of believers even as they are being celebrated in the ritual actions of worship. The sacramental life of the Catholic Church distinguishes it from the many other churches. The sacramental aspect of our religious experience is an essential part of what it means to be a Catholic. A Catholic identity is formed in a significant way by a person's sacramental practice. An understanding of the sacraments of the Church is basic, then, to our very identity as Catholics.

STUDY QUESTIONS

1. What is a sacrament?

"The sacraments are efficacious signs of grace, instituted by Christ and entrusted to the Church, by which divine life is dispensed to us. The visible rites by which the sacraments are celebrated signify and make present the graces proper to each sacrament. They bear fruit in those who receive them with the required dispositions" (CCC 1131). A sacrament is a point of encounter with God; it is the experience of God reaching us and us reaching God.

2. What are the sacraments?

The sacraments are symbolic and ritual acts of worship that draw people more fully under the influence of God's grace. "Celebrated worthily in faith, the sacraments confer the grace that they signify (cf. Council of Trent [1547]: DS 1605; DS 1606). They are *efficacious* because in them Christ himself is at work: it is he who baptizes, he who acts in his sacraments in order to communicate the grace that each sacrament signifies" (CCC 1127). In celebrating the sacraments, we are fundamentally responsive and receptive to God's grace. We are not, however, passive in our celebration and reception of the sacraments. The responsiveness needed to encounter the Lord's initiative is deeply active. In fact, our response is an act of worship like thanksgiving, confession, service, or commitment. Finally, the sacraments are ritual acts of incorporation into the grace and mission of Christ, who continually gathers, strengthens, and commissions his people to carry on that mission.

3. How did the sacraments originate?

The sacraments originated in Christ, just as the Church originated in Christ. "'Adhering to the teaching of the Holy Scriptures, to the apostolic traditions, and to the consensus ... of the Fathers,' we profess that 'the sacraments of the new law were ... all instituted by Jesus Christ our Lord' (Council of Trent [1547]: DS 1600-1601)" (CCC 1114). He did not set the precise rituals for the celebration of the sacraments; neither did he specify the exact organizational structure for the government of the Church. But both the Church and the sacraments find their origin in Christ.

4. What must a person do to celebrate a sacrament?

The person who seeks to receive a sacrament must have the proper disposition, which is faith. "The Holy Spirit prepares the faithful for the sacraments by the Word of God and the faith which welcomes that word in well-disposed hearts. Thus the sacraments strengthen faith and express it" (CCC 1133). The sacraments do not operate magically; rather, they are acts of the whole Church through which a person is drawn more fully into the life and mission of the Church. A person doesn't have to have the deepest or most edifying faith in the world in order to receive a sacrament. In fact, receiving a sacrament may produce the proper disposition.

5. How many sacraments are there?

"There are seven sacraments in the Church: Baptism, Confirmation or Chrismation, Eucharist, Penance, Anointing of the Sick, Holy Orders, and Matrimony (cf. Council of Lyons II [1274]: DS 860; Council of Florence [1439]: DS 1310; Council of Trent [1547]: DS 1601)" (CCC 1113).

6. What are the sacraments of initiation?

The sacraments of initiation are Baptism, Confirmation, and the Eucharist. "Christian initiation is accomplished by three sacraments together: Baptism which is the beginning of new life; Confirmation which is its strengthening; and the Eucharist which nourishes the disciple with Christ's Body and Blood for his transformation in Christ" (CCC 1275). A time of learning and formation usually precedes the adult's celebration of the sacraments of initiation. This period is called the "baptismal catechumenate." Those entering the Catholic Church from most other Christian denominations do not become catechumens and are not ordinarily re-baptized because they are already baptized members of the Body of Christ.

7. *What is the meaning of the sacrament of Baptism?*

"Baptism is birth into the new life in Christ. In accordance with the Lord's will, it is necessary for salvation, as is the Church herself, which we enter by Baptism" (CCC 1277). In Baptism we become the adopted sons and daughters of God, sharers in his own divine life, members of the Body of Christ, and temples of the Holy Spirit. Baptism is also the act of insertion or incorporation into the People of God, who are committed to making the mission of Christ their own mission.

8. *If Baptism is so important, why baptize infants who don't know anything about it?*

Every human being is born into the human condition, which by its very nature includes sin. In Christ this sinful process has been reversed, and in the Church the struggle against evil is carried on by God's people. The baptism of an infant is a commitment on the part of the parents and the whole community of the Church to direct the life of the child away from sin and toward life in Christ. God's love for the infant is made concrete in parental concern to free the infant from the inherited human destiny of sin and to open the infant to a life of grace. In this way, the baptism of infants makes sense as a sacramental celebration of the beginning of life in Christ. "Since the earliest times, Baptism has been administered to children, for it is a grace and a gift of God that does not presuppose any human merit; children are baptized in the faith of the Church" (CCC 1282).

9. *Is Baptism necessary for salvation?*

"The Lord himself affirms that Baptism is necessary for salvation (cf. Jn 3:5). He also commands his disciples to proclaim the Gospel to all nations and to baptize them (cf. Mt 28:19-20; cf. Council of Trent [1547] DS 1618; *LG* 14: *AG* 5). Baptism is necessary for salvation for those to whom the Gospel has been proclaimed and who have had the possibility of asking for this sacrament (cf. Mk 16:16). The Church does not know of any means other than Baptism that assures entry into eternal beatitude; this is why she takes care not to neglect the mission she has received from the Lord to see that all who can be baptized are 'reborn of water and the Spirit.' *God has bound salvation to the sacrament of Baptism, but he himself is not bound by his sacraments*" (CCC 1257).

The Church has always taught that the sacrament of Baptism is necessary for salvation. Those who are convinced that Jesus is Lord must seek admission to his Church through sacramental Baptism. Many are never baptized in their lifetime, however, and God intends the salvation of all. Therefore, baptism of desire, even implicitly experienced by those who never heard of Christ but who want to conform their wills to the will of God, is sufficient for salvation.

10. *What about infants who die un-baptized? Are they saved?*

Infants who die un-baptized are not guilty of any personal sin. Neither have they received God's saving grace. Thomas Aquinas teaches that God will bless such infants with natural happiness. God's love embraces everyone, even if they do not find the way to Baptism or if they have no one to help them find the way. "As regards *children who have died without Baptism*, the Church can only entrust them to the mercy of God, as she does in her funeral rites for them. Indeed, the great mercy of God who desires that all men should be saved, and Jesus' tenderness toward children which caused him to say: 'Let the children come to me, do not hinder them' (Mk 10:14; cf. 1 Tim 2:4), allow us to hope that there is a way of salvation for children who have died without Baptism. All the more urgent is the Church's call not to prevent little children coming to Christ through the gift of holy Baptism" (CCC 1261).

11. *What is the meaning of the sacrament of Confirmation?*

Confirmation is very closely related to Baptism. "Confirmation perfects Baptismal grace; it is the sacrament which gives the Holy Spirit in order to root us more deeply in the divine filiation, incorporate us more firmly into Christ, strengthen our bond with the Church, associate us more closely with her mission, and help us bear witness to the Christian faith in words accompanied by deeds" (CCC 1316). The separate rite of Confirmation allows one who was baptized as an infant to ratify that baptism personally and to accept freely his or her responsibility of service to the Church and the world. When an adult catechumen is baptized, he may also be confirmed immediately to demonstrate the closeness of Baptism and Confirmation and their relation to the mission of the Church.

12. *What is the meaning of the sacrament of the Eucharist?*

"The Eucharist is the heart and the summit of the Church's life, for in it Christ associates his Church and all her members with his sacrifice of praise and thanksgiving offered once for all on the cross to his Father; by this sacrifice he pours out the graces of salvation on his Body which is the Church" (CCC 1407). The word "Eucharist" means "thanksgiving," and its origins lie in the Passover meal that Jesus celebrated with his disciples as he faced his own imminent and innocent death. Jesus identified himself with bread and wine, and he shared bread, broken for all, and wine, poured out for many, with his disciples. He then directed them to continue this action as a memorial of him. The early Church understood this meal as establishing a new covenant in the blood of Christ for the redemption of the world. They pledged to celebrate this memorial of the life, death, and resurrection of Jesus until he would come again. As they had celebrated their passage from the bondage of slavery to freedom in their Passover, so they celebrated their passage from the bondage of sin to the freedom of life in Christ when they celebrated the Eucharist.

The dynamic force of this Eucharistic memorial is a more profound incorporation into Christ's self-sacrifice and a more profound incorporation into the Church. The self-appropriation of the life, death, and resurrection of Jesus is the grace of the sacrament of the Eucharist. The Church is most clearly itself in the Eucharist, as it gathers a people to listen to the Word of God and to share the one bread and the one cup until he comes again.

13. How is Jesus present in the Eucharistic celebration?

Jesus is present first of all in the Eucharistic species, the consecrated bread and wine that are his Body and Blood. He is present in the Word of God that comes from Sacred Scripture and through the homily. He is present in the priest who gathers the community and leads them in prayer. He is also present in the community of people gathered in his name. Within the Eucharistic action, the risen Lord identifies the bread and wine with his own body and blood, thereby conferring on them a new meaning. By this action, the bread and wine are substantially changed and are indeed no longer bread and wine, but truly the Body and Blood of Christ. Therefore, in the Eucharist, Christ is truly present.

14. Why is the Sunday Eucharist so important?

Sunday is the day on which Jesus came forth from the tomb as the firstborn of a whole new creation. Each Sunday commemorates that first Easter Sunday, and Eucharistic commemoration is the most appropriate means of celebration. Sunday is the day when we focus on the future, where our hope rests. Sharing the Eucharist gives a foretaste of that union with God and anticipates our final communion with him in Christ. We are a future-oriented people who long for the return of the Lord. Sunday, the first day of the week, marks our renewed beginning, our minds enlightened by the light of Christ's resurrection. To celebrate precisely what we await on the day it all began seems most appropriate. "The Sunday Eucharist is the foundation and confirmation of all Christian practice. For this reason the faithful are obliged to participate in the Eucharist on days of obligation, unless excused for a serious reason (for example, illness, the care of infants) or dispensed by their own pastor (cf. CIC, can. 1245). Those who deliberately fail in this obligation commit a grave sin" (CCC 2181).

15. What are the sacraments of healing?

"The Lord Jesus Christ, physician of our souls and bodies, who forgave the sins of the paralytic and restored him to bodily health (cf. Mk 2:1-12), has willed that his Church continue, in the power of the Holy Spirit, his work of healing and salvation, even among her own members. This is the purpose of the two sacraments of healing: the sacrament of Penance and the sacrament of Anointing of the Sick" (CCC 1421).

16. What is the meaning of the sacrament of Penance and Reconciliation?

Christians are pilgrims on the way to becoming who God wants us to become. This process of conversion is the context for understanding the sacrament of Penance. When a person becomes distant from God or his relationship with God becomes strained or broken through sin, celebrating the sacrament of Penance sharply focuses the sinner's need for forgiveness and God's loving response. If the sinner has broken with God in a fundamental way, the Church extends God's mercy and invites the sinner to the Lord's Table again, pledging her support in the process of conversion. If the person's relationship with God is merely strained and not broken, the Church acts to encourage a still more clearly focused orientation of the person's heart to God.

The Second Vatican Council teaches, "Those who approach the sacrament of Penance obtain pardon from God's mercy for the offense committed against him, and are, at the same time, reconciled with the Church which they have wounded by their sins and which by charity, by example, and by prayer labors for their conversion" (*Dogmatic Constitution on the Church*, 11).

17. *Is the sacrament of Penance and Reconciliation the only way sins committed after Baptism are forgiven?*

The sacrament of Penance and Reconciliation is not the only way sins are forgiven after Baptism. The Christian life is a process of conversion away from the self and toward God. It is a process of surrender of the self to God and a consequent deepening of our love for God. Whatever facilitates this movement toward God brings about the forgiveness of sins. The Fathers of the Church "cite as means of obtaining forgiveness of sins: efforts at reconciliation with one's neighbor, tears of repentance, concern for the salvation of one's neighbor, the intercession of the saints, and the practice of charity" (CCC 1434). Appropriating the mission of Christ to one's self in receiving the Eucharist, a prayer of genuine sorrow, a particular work of penance, or a sincere celebration of the penitential rite at the beginning of Mass are important ways of obtaining forgiveness for venial sin. If, however, we have committed mortal sin, we need to seek God's forgiveness and reconciliation with the Church in the sacrament of Penance.

18. *Why do we have to confess our sins to a priest?*

We have to confess our sins to a priest if we seek to celebrate the sacrament of Penance or if we have sinned mortally and seek God's forgiveness. The priest, as God's instrument and official representative of the Church, pronounces the solemn assurance that God's grace transforms the sinner's heart and restores the sinner again as an adopted daughter or son of God. "One who desires to obtain reconciliation with God and with the Church must confess to a priest all the unconfessed grave sins he remembers after having carefully examined his conscience. The confession of venial faults, without being necessary in itself, is nevertheless strongly recommended by the Church" (CCC 1493).

19. *What is the meaning of the sacrament of the Anointing of the Sick?*

The sacrament of the Anointing of the Sick is a sign of Christ's loving concern for a sick member of the Church and a celebration of the healing presence of Christ in the midst of his people. The sacrament of the Anointing of the Sick is not merely a demonstration of concern. "The sacrament of Anointing of the Sick has as its purpose the conferral of a special grace on the Christian experiencing the difficulties inherent in the condition of grave illness or old age" (CCC 1527). Therefore, illness does not remain an opportunity to turn in on one's self, but rather becomes an opportunity to be one with Christ in his suffering, confident of his ultimate victory over suffering and death. This healing grace of the sacrament of the Anointing of the Sick helps the person grow through the sickness and suffering to an even deeper level of incorporation into the life of the Church.

20. *What are the sacraments at the service of communion?*

"Two other sacraments, Holy Orders and Matrimony, are directed towards the salvation of others; if they contribute as well to personal salvation, it is through service to others that they do so. They confer a particular mission in the Church and serve to build up the People of God" (CCC 1534). Holy Orders and Matrimony are the sacraments at the service of communion.

21. What is the meaning of the sacrament of Holy Orders?

The sacrament of Holy Orders attends to the order of the Church and ensures that the Church will act sacramentally in proclaiming the Word of God, celebrating the sacraments, and continuing the mission of Christ. The sacrament of Holy Orders incorporates the person into the body of those with ministerial responsibility and authority in the Church. This is not to say that only ordained ministers have responsibility and authority in the Church, but rather that ordained ministers have the particular and primary responsibility of service to the Church. "The ministerial priesthood differs in essence from the common priesthood of the faithful because it confers a sacred power for the service of the faithful. The ordained ministers exercise their service for the People of God by teaching (*munus docendi*), divine worship (*munus liturgicum*) and pastoral governance (*munus regendi*)" (CCC 1592).

The sacrament of Holy Orders designates and consecrates a man for leadership in the Church. He does not assume this responsibility on his own but is called by the Holy Spirit, approved by the People of God, and sealed by sacramental orders to continue Christ's mission. The grace of the sacrament of Holy Orders empowers the deacon, priest, or bishop to live a life of dedicated service in the Church and enables him, insofar as he cooperates with that grace, to build up the Body of Christ by celebrating the sacraments faithfully, preaching the Gospel boldly, and being present to his people completely.

22. What is the meaning of the sacrament of Matrimony?

In the sacrament of Matrimony, each partner freely bestows upon the other a covenant that is not merely an exchange of rights and duties, but an exchange of persons. Christian marriage is the human pledge of lifelong love and exclusive fidelity that is a sign of the divine pledge of enduring love by which God bestowed himself on the people of Israel. The sacrament of Matrimony seals this covenant before God, who is its author and witness. The couple's pledge of covenant love is made at the deepest level of their freedom and fundamentally directs their lives in a self-forgetting way that is rooted in the redemptive love of Christ. The fullest expression of this sacramental love is sexual union, the intense personal self-bestowal of the man upon the woman and of the woman upon the man, which opens them both to the creation of new life.

"The sacrament of Matrimony signifies the union of Christ and the Church. It gives spouses the grace to love each other with the love with which Christ has loved his Church; the grace of the sacrament thus perfects the human love of the spouses, strengthens their indissoluble unity, and sanctifies them on the way to eternal life (c.f. Council of Trent: DS 1799)" (CCC 1661).

23. *What is a sacramental?*

A sacramental is a blessed object or action used in conjunction with the rites of the Church in order to invoke God's blessing and help. "Sacramentals are sacred signs instituted by the Church. They prepare men to receive the fruit of the sacraments and sanctify different circumstances of life" (CCC 1677). Some examples of sacramentals are holy water, blessed candles, statues, crucifixes, and medals.

24. *When are sacramentals used?*

Holy water is available when a person enters a Catholic church or some Catholic homes. The person may dip the tips of the fingers in the holy water and trace the sign of Christ's cross from the forehead to the heart and the shoulders. Blessed candles are often used by the Church to represent the presence of Christ, the light of the world. They are used at Mass, at baptisms, at anointings, and at Christian burials, among other times. Blessed palm is given to Catholics on Palm Sunday and is often kept in Catholic homes throughout the year as a sign of the Passion of Jesus. Blessed ashes are made from the blessed palms and are imposed on the foreheads of Catholics on Ash Wednesday, the beginning of Lent, to signify the frailty of humanity and the Catholic's willingness to do penance during Lent in conjunction with the sufferings of Christ. Statues in churches or Catholic homes honor Mary, the Mother of God, or the particular saint whom they resemble. Crucifixes in churches or Catholic homes honor Christ as the Redeemer of the world. Medals worn by Catholics honor Christ, the saint, or the holy person inscribed thereon.

25. What are the origin, purpose, and role of sacramentals in the Church?
From ancient times, the Church has set certain objects and actions apart as points of encounter for the person and God. Sacramentals, the Second Vatican Council teaches, "are sacred signs which bear a resemblance to the sacraments. They signify effects, particularly of a spiritual nature, which are obtained through the intercession of the Church. By them men are disposed to receive the chief effect of the sacraments, and various occasions in life are rendered holy" (*Constitution on the Sacred Liturgy*, 60). Sacramentals supplement the sacraments; they in no way replace the sacraments. Sacramentals cause grace primarily because of the faith and devotion of those who are using, receiving, or celebrating the sacramental. "Among sacramentals *blessings* (of persons, meals, objects, and places) come first. Every blessing praises God and prays for his gifts. In Christ, Christians are blessed by God the Father 'with every spiritual blessing' (Eph 1:3). This is why the Church imparts blessings by invoking the name of Jesus, usually while making the holy sign of the cross of Christ" (CCC 1671).

QUESTIONS FOR GROUP DISCUSSION

1. Are the sacraments personal or communal experiences of God's love?
2. Does receiving the sacraments constitute the whole of religious life for Catholics?
3. How do the sacraments give grace?
4. Why are there only seven sacraments?
5. How do God's offer of love and the individual's response in faith work in the sacraments?

QUESTIONS FOR PERSONAL REFLECTION

1. Am I aware of the natural signs of God's presence in the world?
2. What sign of God's presence is particularly important to me?
3. Are celebrations of the sacraments for me personal experiences of God's saving love?
4. Do the sacraments unite me with the wider community of the Church?

PRAYER TO IMITATE JESUS

Have among yourselves the same attitude that is also yours in Christ Jesus,

Who, though he was in the form of God,
did not regard equality with God something to be grasped.
Rather, he emptied himself,
taking the form of a slave,
coming in human likeness;
and found human in appearance,
he humbled himself,
becoming obedient to death,
even death on a cross.
Because of this, God greatly exalted him
and bestowed on him the name
that is above every name,
that at the name of Jesus
every knee should bend,
of those in heaven and on earth and under the earth,
and every tongue confess that
Jesus Christ is Lord,
to the glory of God the Father.

PHILIPPIANS 2:5-11

CHAPTER 16

Ecclesial Lay Ministry

―――

SCRIPTURE REFLECTION

There are different kinds of spiritual gifts but the same Spirit; there are different forms of service but the same Lord; there are different workings but the same God who produces all of them in everyone. To each individual the manifestation of the Spirit is given for some benefit. To one is given through the Spirit the expression of wisdom; to another the expression of knowledge according to the same Spirit; to another faith by the same Spirit; to another gifts of healing by the one Spirit; to another mighty deeds; to another prophecy; to another discernment of spirits; to another varieties of tongues; to another interpretation of tongues. But one and the same Spirit produces all of these, distributing them individually to each person as he wishes.

1 CORINTHIANS 12:4-11

INTRODUCTION

Since the Second Vatican Council, there has been an expansion of the notion of ecclesial lay ministry in the Church. The documents of that council emphasized the baptismal vocation of all believers to live out what the council Fathers called the "common priesthood of the faithful." The increased involvement of lay people in the ministries of the Church since the council has been most dramatic. Lay people now hold important administrative positions in diocesan offices as well as in parishes. Lay people serve the Church as chancellors, superintendents of diocesan education offices, directors of diocesan catechetical programs, teachers, catechists, and educational volunteers of every kind. In addition, lay Catholics participate in liturgical ministry, social justice ministry, personnel administration, financial management, religious publication, and in the matrimonial tribunals of the Church. The mission of the Church in the United States depends a great deal on the active response of the laity to their baptismal commitment.

STUDY QUESTIONS

1. *What does the term "laity" mean?*

   The Second Vatican Council's *Dogmatic Constitution on the Church* states, "The term 'laity' is here understood to mean all the faithful except those in Holy Orders and those who belong to a religious state approved by the Church. That is, the faithful, who by Baptism are incorporated into Christ and integrated into the People of God, are made sharers in their particular way in the priestly, prophetic, and kingly office of Christ, and have their own part to play in the mission of the whole Christian people in the Church and in the world" (n. 31).

2. *What is the vocation of the laity?*

   God calls lay people to seek his Kingdom by engaging in secular and temporal affairs and directing them, as far as possible, according to God's loving plan of salvation for all people. Their vocation is to permeate the social, political, and economic realities of the world with the message and mission of Christ. "Since, like all the faithful, lay Christians are entrusted by God with the apostolate by virtue of their Baptism and Confirmation, they have the right and duty, individually or grouped in associations, to work so that the divine message of salvation may be known and accepted by all men throughout the earth. This duty is the more pressing when it is only through them that men can hear the Gospel and know Christ. Their activity in ecclesial communities is so necessary that, for the most part, the apostolate of pastors cannot be fully effective without it (cf. *LG* 33)" (CCC 900).

3. *What is ministry?*

Ministry is the service of sanctification given in the preaching of the Word of God and in the celebration of the sacraments by those in Holy Orders and in certain circumstance by the laity. Since Christ gave the Church her authority and mission, he is the source of all ministry in the Church and all ministry is offered in his name. The Second Vatican Council's *Decree on the Apostolate of the Laity* teaches, "In the Church there is a diversity of ministry but a oneness of mission. Christ conferred on the apostles and their successors the duty of teaching, sanctifying, and ruling in his name and power. But the laity likewise share in the priestly, prophetic and royal office of Christ and therefore have their own share in the mission of the whole People of God in the Church and in the world" (n. 2).

4. *What is ecclesial lay ministry, then?*

Ecclesial lay ministry is the participation of the lay faithful in the priestly, prophetic, and kingly offices of Christ. It is service given in the name of Christ by lay people who have been prepared for a particular ministry and sanctioned for that ministry by the Church.

5. *How do ecclesial lay ministers participate in the priestly office of Christ?*

Ecclesial lay ministers participate in the priestly office of Christ especially when they are "admitted permanently to the ministries of lector and acolyte" (cf. CIC, can. 230 § 1) (CCC 903). In certain circumstances and with proper approval, lay people can also exercise the ministry of the Word, preside over liturgical prayers, confer Baptism, and distribute Holy Communion in accord with the prescriptions of law.

6. *How do ecclesial lay ministers participate in the prophetic office of Christ?*
Ecclesial lay ministers participate in the prophetic office of Christ
when they bear witness to the Gospel of Christ, especially through
their efforts in evangelization — that is, the proclamation of Christ
to unbelievers as well as to the faithful. "Lay people who are capable and trained may also collaborate in catechetical formation, in
teaching the sacred sciences, and in the use of the communications
media" (cf. CIC, cann. 229; 774; 776; 780; 823 § 1) (CCC 906).

7. *How do ecclesial lay ministers participate in the kingly office of Christ?*
Ecclesial lay ministers participate in the kingly office of Christ
when they are called to cooperate with their pastors in enhancing
the life of the ecclesial community and in providing for its growth.
"In the Church, 'lay members of the Christian faithful can cooperate in the exercise of the power [of governance] in accord with the
norm of law' (CIC, can. 129 § 2). And so the Church provides for
their presence at particular councils, diocesan synods, pastoral
councils; the exercise of the pastoral care of a parish, collaboration
in finance committees, and participation in ecclesial tribunals, etc.
(cf. CIC, cann. 443 § 4; 463 §§ 1 and 2; 492 § 1; 511; 517 § 2; 536;
1421 § 2)" (CCC 911).

8. *What is the relationship between lay ministers and ordained ministers?*
Those in Holy Orders and ecclesial lay ministers share the same
baptismal vocation to ministry and therefore share in Christ's
priesthood. However, the common priesthood of all the faithful
and the ministerial or hierarchical priesthood are not the same.
"The ministerial or hierarchical priesthood of bishops and priests,
and the common priesthood of all the faithful participate, 'each in
its own proper way, in the one priesthood of Christ.' While being
'ordered one to another,' they differ essentially (*LG*, 10 § 2)" (CCC
1547). They should work together in a collaborative manner that
emphasizes the cooperation essential to the unity that is theirs in

Christ. Often this collaborative style of ministry is deepened and enhanced through regular and common prayer between ecclesial lay ministers and the ordained.

9. *In what sense do the common priesthood of all the faithful and the ministerial or hierarchical priesthood differ essentially?*

They differ essentially because the faithful exercise the priesthood of Christ in common by virtue of their Baptism in order to live a holy life. Members of the ministerial or hierarchical priesthood exercise the priesthood of Christ by virtue of their sacramental ordination. "The ministerial priesthood is at the service of the common priesthood. It is directed at the unfolding of the baptismal grace of all Christians. The ministerial priesthood is a *means* by which Christ unceasingly builds up and leads his Church. For this reason it is transmitted by its own sacrament, the sacrament of Holy Orders" (CCC 1547).

10. *Do ecclesial lay ministers need special training?*

Since all ministry is given in the name of Christ, the gift of faith in Jesus Christ and a fruitful experience of Christian life are basic to ministry of any kind. Depending on the particular ministry, however, special skills may be needed. For example, teachers and catechists need specific training in child development and educational methods, while a pastoral minister needs specific training in visiting the sick, accompanying the dying, counseling the bereaved, caring for the poor, working with the handicapped, etc.

11. *What about the role of religious sisters and brothers in ministry?*

"Religious life derives from the mystery of the Church. It is a gift she has received from her Lord, a gift she offers as a stable way of life to the faithful called by God to profess the counsels. Thus, the Church can both show forth Christ and acknowledge herself to be the Savior's bride. Religious life in its various forms is called to signify the very charity of God in the language of our time" (CCC

926). Technically, sisters and brothers are members of the laity because they are not ordained. Because they publicly profess the evangelical counsels of poverty, chastity, and obedience, however, they are distinct from the laity as well. They most often serve in the name of Christ as teachers, administrators, nurses, social workers, and pastoral ministers, as well as in many other ministerial roles.

12. *What is the special contribution of women and men in consecrated life?*
The consecrated life is an irreplaceable element in the life and holiness of the Church. It is a unique way of consecrating oneself to God's service and to the good of the Church, of dedicating oneself to follow Christ, and of signifying in the Church the coming glory of the Kingdom of God. "In the Church, which is like the sacrament — the sign and instrument — of God's own life, the consecrated life is seen as a special sign of the mystery of redemption. To follow and imitate Christ more nearly and to manifest more clearly his self-emptying is to be more deeply present to one's contemporaries, in the heart of Christ" (CCC 932).

QUESTIONS FOR GROUP DISCUSSION

1. Why have lay people become so active in the Church?
2. Will lay people be ministering in situations usually reserved for priests?
3. Do some people have difficulty accepting lay people as ministers?
4. Do lay people have any real power in the Church?
5. What does baptismal calling or vocation mean to the average Christian?

QUESTIONS FOR PERSONAL REFLECTION

1. Do I understand that my baptismal call is a call to share the common priesthood of the faithful?
2. What is my attitude toward the ecclesial lay ministers in my parish?

3. How do I give service in the name of the Lord?

4. Have I given serious consideration to offering my services as a minister in my parish?

PRAYER OF THANKSGIVING FOR JESUS

[Let us give] thanks to the Father, who has made you fit to share in the inheritance of the holy ones in light. He delivered us from the power of darkness and transferred us to the kingdom of his beloved Son, in whom we have redemption, the forgiveness of sins.

He is the image of the invisible God,
   the firstborn of all creation.
For in him were created all things in heaven and on earth,
   the visible and the invisible,
   whether thrones or dominions or principalities or powers;
   all things were created through him and for him.
He is before all things,
   and in him all things hold together.
He is the head of the body, the church.
He is the beginning, the firstborn from the dead,
   that in all things he himself might be preeminent.
For in him all the fullness was pleased to dwell,
   and through him to reconcile all things for him,
   making peace by the blood of his cross,
   [through him], whether those on earth or those in heaven.

COLOSSIANS 1:12-20

The Family of the Church

SCRIPTURE REFLECTION

I, then, a prisoner for the Lord, urge you to live in a manner worthy of the call you have received, with all humility and gentleness, with patience, bearing with one another through love, striving to preserve the unity of the spirit through the bond of peace: one body and one Spirit, as you were also called to the one hope of your call; one Lord, one faith, one baptism; one God and Father of all, who is over all and through all and in all.

EPHESIANS 4:1-6

INTRODUCTION

A family is a community of mutual respect and support, a circle of concern and encouragement, and an interdependent enterprise of commitment and service. Its bond is love. The Church is the family of God's favored people formed by the Holy Spirit as the Body of Christ. Her bond is Jesus, the model of love.

Just as a parent lovingly accepts a child from God, so God adopts us as his own. Just as a parent proudly embraces a child, so God enfolds each of us in his arms. A parent carefully bestows a name on a child; God calls each of us by name. A parent nurtures a child through life; God attends to us with his eternal love.

The family molds its unique identity partially around the family table and expresses that identity in its table prayer. The Church celebrates its identity around the Table of the Lord and expresses that identity in the memorial sacrifice of the Eucharist. As family members depend on one another to develop a sense of family history, continuity, and loyalty, so does the Church depend on her members to share the vitality and enthusiasm of the Holy Spirit. It is the Holy Spirit who forms, enlivens, and guides the Church.

As family members turn to one another for compassion and understanding in times of trouble, so does the Church, our Mother and Teacher, gather us to help one another in our struggle to make the best of God's gifts of life and faith.

Service to one another and to the world is the challenge to both the family unit and the Church, the family of God. A family that is turned in on itself, caring only for its own needs and protecting only its own interests, is an unhealthy family. As family members place their gifts at the service of one another, so the Church places her gifts at the service of the world. The mission of the family is to provide an environment of love and concern in which its members can themselves become providers of love and concern for others. The mission of the Church is to evangelize — that is, to proclaim the Good News of Jesus' love and concern and to embody his presence in this world.

STUDY QUESTIONS

1. *Why is the Church called the "People of God"?*
   "People of God" is an Old Testament metaphor for God's Chosen People, Israel. Christ instituted a New Covenant and constituted a new People of God. "Jesus Christ is the one whom the Father anointed with the Holy Spirit and established as priest, prophet, and king. The whole People of God participates in these three offices of Christ and bears the responsibilities for mission and service that

flow from them (cf. John Paul II, *RH* 18-21)" (CCC 783). The People of God are "a chosen race, a royal priesthood, a holy nation, a people of his own" (1 Pt 2:9). They are chosen by God to be his people; they are reborn in water and the Spirit by faith and Baptism; they have the dignity and freedom of the children of God; they have been given the new commandment to love as Christ loved; they have been entrusted with Christ's mission to proclaim the coming of the Kingdom; and they are destined to live in communion with God. In these senses, the Church is the People of God.

2. *Why is the Church called the "Body of Christ"?*

A body is an interdependent organism, not merely an assortment of parts. St. Paul used this image frequently in his letters to teach that the Church is a living and interrelated community in which a diversity of roles serves the central unity of the whole body. The Church is the Body of Christ because Christ established the community of believers as his own Body. He accomplished this through the Holy Spirit and his actions in the sacraments, especially the Eucharist. "The Church is this Body of which Christ is the head: she lives from him, in him, and for him; he lives with her and in her" (CCC 807)

3. *Why is the Church called the "Bride of Christ"?*

The relationship that exists between Christ and the Church, unity in distinction, is akin to that of a bridegroom and bride. Sacred Scripture attests to this, especially when Christ refers to himself as the "bridegroom" (Mk 2:19). "The Church is the Bride of Christ: he loved her and handed himself over for her. He has purified her by his blood and made her the fruitful mother of all God's children" (CCC 808).

4. *Why is the Church called the "Temple of the Holy Spirit"?*

The Holy Spirit is the principle of life in the Church, the Body of Christ. He constitutes the Body by the Word of God; he breathes life into the Body by Baptism; he continually forms the Body through the sacraments; he builds up the Body in charity; he strengthens the members for Christ's mission; he directs the Body to the good by the virtues; and he sustains the Body by special graces.

"The Church is the Temple of the Holy Spirit. The Spirit is the soul, as it were, of the Mystical Body, the source of its life, of its unity in diversity, and of the riches of its gifts and charisms" (CCC 809).

5. *How best does the Church celebrate its "family" life?*
The Church most fully expresses herself as a family, as a community of love, in the celebration of the Eucharist. In the Eucharistic liturgy, the Word of God is proclaimed, the Church's faith is shared, the saving action of Jesus is made present, the community of believers is nourished by the Body and Blood of Christ, and the members are sent on Christ's mission to proclaim the coming of the Kingdom. St. Paul asked, "The cup of blessing that we bless, is it not a participation in the blood of Christ? The bread that we break, is it not a participation in the body of Christ? Because the loaf of bread is one, we, though many, are one body, for we all partake of the one loaf" (1 Cor 10:16-17).

6. *What part does the individual Christian play in the life of the Church?*
The mission of the Church, to proclaim the Good News of the Kingdom, is the responsibility of the whole Church. Each Christian is consecrated as "another Christ" by Baptism. The Second Vatican Council's *Decree on the Apostolate of the Laity* teaches, "The characteristic of the lay state being a life led in the midst of the world and of secular affairs, lay people are called by God to make of their apostolate, through the vigor of their Christian spirit, a leaven in the world" (n. 2). In our homes we sanctify the day with prayer,

relate to one another with respect, share our faith in Christ, and model Christian behavior. In our work we appreciate the dignity of our labor, help fellow workers, are honest and just in business, and render a just day's work for a just wage. In our social life we are responsible citizens, work for justice and peace, respect the dignity of human life in all its forms, and treat everyone with justice and mercy.

7. What is a saint?

A saint is a holy person who, through the grace of Christ, leads a life in union with God and receives the reward of eternal life with him. Some holy persons have been solemnly proclaimed saints because they practiced heroic virtue and lived in fidelity to God's grace. "The Church recognizes the power of the Spirit of holiness within her and sustains the hope of believers by proposing the saints to them as models and intercessors" (cf. *LG* 40; 48-51) (CCC 828). The process by which a person is formally declared a saint is called "canonization."

8. What is the role of the saints in the Church?

The Church honors the saints for the example of their virtuous lives. They are models of faith; they are models of Christian virtue. They remind us of our true destiny and inspire us to persevere in our love of God and one another. In imitating the saints, we imitate Jesus, who is their model and ours. Since they are already closely united to Christ, the saints also intercede for us before the Father. "The witnesses who have preceded us into the kingdom (cf. Heb 12:1), especially those whom the Church recognizes as saints, share in the living tradition of prayer by the example of their lives, the transmission of their writings, and their prayer today. They contemplate God, praise him and constantly care for those whom they have left on earth" (CCC 2683).

9. *Who are some of the saints, and what are the Christian virtues they witness?*

Mary, the mother of Jesus, and Joseph, her husband, are preeminent models of faith because of their respective unique relationships with Christ. Peter, Andrew, James, John, Philip, Bartholomew, Matthew, Thomas, James (son of Alphaeus), Simon, Jude, and Matthias were apostles and pastors. They witnessed the virtues of wisdom, selflessness, fidelity, and courage as they established the early churches and faced death for their beliefs.

Martyrs, like Stephen, Agnes, Agatha, Justin, Lucy, Cecilia, Vincent, Denis, Thomas Becket, Thomas More, John Fisher, Isaac Jogues, John Brebeuf, Charles Lwanga, Andrew Kim, Paul Chong Hasang, Teresa Benedicta of the Cross, and Andrew Dung-Lac gave up their lives rather than their faith.

Augustine, Thomas Aquinas, Bede, Bonaventure, Ignatius of Antioch, and Robert Bellarmine were great teachers of the faith and witnessed the significance of spiritual learning in the Church.

Paul of Tarsus, Patrick, Paul Miki, Augustine of Canterbury, Boniface, Cyril, Peter Chanel, and Francis Xavier were fearless missionaries who were singularly committed to extend the Gospel to every nation.

The dignity of labor is the witness of Joseph the Worker and Isidore. Francis Xavier Cabrini, Joan of Arc, and Peter Claver stood firmly for social justice. Francis and Clare of Assisi, Elizabeth of Hungary, and Catherine of Siena dedicated themselves to peace.

An extraordinary love for the poor was shown by Vincent de Paul, Stanislaus, Raymond of Peñafort, Frances of Rome, Margaret of Scotland, and Louis of France. Nicholas, John Vianney, and Maximilian Kolbe witnessed exceptional charity. Benedict, Dominic, Anthony, Paul of the Cross, Angela Merici, Columban, Alphonsus Ligouri, Peter Julian Eymard, Ignatius Loyola, Bridget,

Basil, and Francis de Sales started religious orders bound to poverty, chastity, and obedience. Thérèse of Lisieux, Martin de Porres, Rita of Cascia, Kateri Tekakwitha, Peter Claver, and Josephine Bakhita dedicated themselves to poverty of spirit and the simple life.

Elizabeth Seton, John Newman, Charles Borromeo, Katharine Drexel, John Bosco, and John Baptist de la Salle witnessed the value of Catholic education. An exceptional care for the study of Scripture was shown by Jerome, Gregory Nazianzen, and Ephrem. Anthony, Athanasius, Cyril of Jerusalem, Cyril of Alexandria, Gregory the Great, Leo the Great, and John Chrysostom stood for the integrity of the authentic doctrine of the Church against heresy.

Teresa of Ávila, Methodius, John of the Cross, and Rose of Lima were profound mystics whose lives testified to the value of prayer.

10. Are there un-canonized saints?

Canonization is a solemn proclamation by the Pope that a deceased member of the faithful may be venerated as a model and intercessor for the whole Christian faithful. In the broadest sense, a saint is one who is united with God in eternity. Therefore, we can assume that there are many un-canonized saints in heaven.

QUESTIONS FOR GROUP DISCUSSION

1. How can the Church be an effective community of love in the world today?
2. What are the signs that the Church is truly a family?
3. Do lay people really play an important part in the life of the Church?
4. Why are there relatively few vocations to the priesthood and religious life?
5. Why does the Church venerate the saints?

QUESTIONS FOR PERSONAL REFLECTION

1. Do I feel I am an integral part of the Body of Christ?
2. What do I really like about my local parish?
3. Would I want my son or daughter to pursue a vocation to the religious life?
4. Who are the heroes or heroines in my life?

PRAYER FOR ALL OF THE FAITHFUL

For this reason I kneel before the Father, from whom every family in heaven and on earth is named, that he may grant you in accord with the riches of his glory to be strengthened with power through his Spirit in the inner self, and that Christ may dwell in your hearts through faith; that you, rooted and grounded in love, may have strength to comprehend with all the holy ones what is the breadth and length and height and depth, and to know the love of Christ that surpasses knowledge, so that you may be filled with all the fullness of God.

Now to him who is able to accomplish far more than all we ask or imagine, by the power at work within us, to him be glory in the church and in Christ Jesus to all generations, forever and ever. Amen.

EPHESIANS 3:14-21

PART THREE

Catholic Practice

In addition to believing and trusting, faith also involves doing. It is Catholic action in the most fundamental sense of that term. Action based on believing the truth God has revealed and on trusting the God who reveals that truth can be called "personal commitment." Our personal commitment is literally the embodiment of our believing and trusting. Personal commitment is a work of the total person. The emphasis in this dimension of faith is on action — deeds of love undertaken precisely because we believe and trust. In his Letter to the Galatians, St. Paul emphasizes faith in action: "For in Christ Jesus, neither circumcision nor uncircumcision counts for anything, but only faith working through love" (Gal 5:6). Charity, justice, mercy, peace, compassion, and understanding are not passive virtues but genuine endeavors to love God by loving our neighbor. Deeds done in light of our personal commitment incorporate what we think we believe and how much we feel we can trust. Personal commitment brings what we say and what we do into a unity. Without action in Jesus' name, faith masquerades as mere information, false security, or superstition. Inactive faith is not faith at all but mere fantasy.

In summary, then, faith is not an abstraction, empty of reason, passion, and obligation. Faith is a synthesis of belief, trust, and personal commitment.

So far, our exploration of the Catholic faith has concentrated on what Catholics believe and how Catholics approach life. But authentic faith needs to be expressed in the day-to-day lives of real people. Our beliefs and our attitudes are embodied in our decisions and lifestyles. Since faith is the full acceptance of Christian responsibility, belief and trust need an outlet. That outlet is integrated Christian living.

Christian life unfolds where it is lived: in offices, parking lots, supermarkets, gymnasiums, shopping malls, factories, backyards, and classrooms. Christian life is not detached from the world, but immersed in its ebb and flow.

The home is the primary setting for living out Christian values. Family bonds provide the fundamental relationships for us to practice the Catholic faith. The family, as Pope Paul VI said, is the "church of the home." The community of believers that is the Catholic Church, however, also affords us a loving environment and other people with whom to share our beliefs, trust, and personal commitment.

In this last section we will explore the sacramental and prayer life of the Catholic faith. The nitty-gritty details of sacramental celebration, prayer in the Catholic tradition, and other practices common to Catholics are described.

The Sacraments of Initiation

- **Baptism** — addresses the questions of who may be baptized, how one baptizes, who may be godparents, and the value of proper baptismal preparation of the parents.
- **Confirmation** — focuses on the requirements for Confirmation and for being a sponsor to the one being confirmed.

- **Eucharist** — responds to questions about the necessity to fast from food and drink before receiving Communion, non-Catholics and Communion, as well as when and how often one should receive Communion.

The Sacraments of Healing

- **Penance and Reconciliation** — deals with the concerns about the requirements for celebrating the sacrament of Penance and Reconciliation, how to go about it, when one should go to confession, and when one must go to confession.
- **Anointing of the Sick** — deals with the requirements for celebrating the sacrament of the Anointing of the Sick, the frequency of its celebration, and its relationship to the "last rites."

The Sacraments at the Service of Communion

- **Holy Orders** — treats questions about the requirements for ordination to the priesthood, the question of women priests, and celibacy.
- **Matrimony** — responds to questions about the freedom to marry and questions about divorce, annulments, and the mechanics of having a bond of marriage investigated by a marriage tribunal.

CHAPTER 18

Baptism

═══

SCRIPTURE REFLECTION

Are you unaware that we who were baptized into Christ Jesus were baptized into his death? We were indeed buried with him through baptism into death, so that, just as Christ was raised from the dead by the glory of the Father, we too might live in newness of life.

For if we have grown into union with him through a death like his, we shall also be united with him in the resurrection.

ROMANS 6:3-5

INTRODUCTION

In the early Church, the ancient ritual of Baptism by immersion (plunging the whole body into the water) signified the burial and resurrection of Christ. The one to be baptized waded into a pool of water, was covered by the baptismal waters, and then emerged from under the water into a whole new way of life, life in Christ. St. Paul says, "All of you who were baptized into Christ have clothed yourselves with Christ" (Gal 3:27).

From the earliest days of Christianity, the Church has baptized both infants and adults. Since Baptism marks the person's participation in God's own life and membership in the Body of Christ, the parents and godparents of infants have the serious responsibility to form the children in the beliefs and practices of the Catholic Church.

The natural sign of water is used in the sacrament of Baptism to cleanse and to give life. Just as natural water cleanses and sustains natural life, so do the sacramental waters of Baptism wash sin away and bestow God's own life. The baptized are incorporated into the life of the Church and become new creations through water and the Spirit.

STUDY QUESTIONS

1. Who may be baptized?

Any person who has faith and a desire to be baptized may be baptized. Infants and young children should be baptized with the permission of a parent or guardian. "Since the earliest times, Baptism has been administered to children, for it is a grace and a gift of God that does not presuppose any human merit; children are baptized in the faith of the Church. Entry into Christian life gives access to true freedom" (CCC 1282). From the beginning, the baptism of adults has been the common practice in those situations where the message of the Gospel has not been received. The baptismal catechumenate occupies an especially important place in these circumstances. This initiation into Christian faith and life should dispose the catechumen to receive the gift of God in Baptism, Confirmation, and the Eucharist.

2. Who is the minister of Baptism?

"The ordinary ministers of Baptism are the bishop and priest and, in the Latin Church, also the deacon (cf. CIC, can. 861 § 1; CCEO, can. 677 § 1). In case of necessity, anyone, even a non-baptized person, with the required intention, can baptize (CIC, can. 861 § 2), by using the Trinitarian baptismal formula. The intention required is to will to do what the Church does when she baptizes. The Church finds the reason for this possibility in the universal saving will of

God and the necessity of Baptism for salvation (cf. 1 Tim 2:4)" (CCC 1256).

3. *How does one baptize?*

"The essential rite of Baptism consists in immersing the candidate in water or pouring water on his head" (CCC 1278), while saying: "I baptize you in the name of the Father, and of the Son, and of the Holy Spirit."

4. *If someone is baptized in an emergency, should the person later be re-baptized?*

No, Baptism is once and for all. "Baptism imprints on the soul an indelible spiritual sign, the character, which consecrates the baptized person for Christian worship. Because of the character Baptism cannot be repeated" (cf. DS 1609 and DS 1624) (CCC 1280). If one was baptized in an emergency, the person should be brought to the church to have the ceremonies surrounding the actual pouring of the water celebrated and the Baptism duly recorded in the parish baptismal register.

5. *Who may be godparents?*

Ordinarily, two practicing Catholics over 14 years of age may be godparents. However, a non-Catholic Christian may replace one of the Catholics and stand as a Christian witness. Godparents accept the responsibility, along with the parents, to provide formation in faith for their godchild. "For the grace of Baptism to unfold, the parents' help is important. So too is the role of the *godfather* and *godmother*, who must be firm believers, able and ready to help the newly baptized — child or adult — on the road of Christian life (cf. CIC, cann. 872-874). Their task is a truly ecclesial function (*officium*) (cf. *SC* 67). The whole ecclesial community bears some responsibility for the development and safeguarding of the grace given at Baptism" (CCC 1255).

6. *Are all Christian baptisms valid?*

Ordinarily, yes. Baptism with water using the Trinitarian formula is necessary. "Baptism constitutes the foundation of communion among all Christians, including those who are not yet in full communion with the Catholic Church" (CCC 1271). One who leaves another part of Christianity to become a Catholic is ordinarily not re-baptized unless there is a prudent doubt about the validity of the prior baptism. Instead, he or she is received into full communion with the Catholic Church after a suitable period of preparation in accord with the directives given in the *Rite of Christian Initiation of Adults.*

7. *Do parents have to be married in the Catholic Church in order to have their children baptized Catholic?*

Baptism is necessary for salvation, so all Christian parents should present their children to the Church for Baptism. "The Church and parents would deny a child the priceless grace of becoming a child of God were they not to confer Baptism shortly after birth" (cf. CIC, can. 867; CCEO, cann. 681; 686, 1) (CCC 1250). For her part, the Church must have a prudent hope that the child will be raised a Catholic in order to baptize the child and must provide assistance to the parents in carrying out this responsibility.

8. *Do parents have to go to classes in order to have their child baptized?*

Sacramental preparation for the parents of a child to be baptized is very important and is ordinarily provided by the local parish. Parents are strongly encouraged to participate in programs of preparation for the baptism of their children. It is their responsibility to rear their children in the faith that they receive at Baptism. Attendance at classes, while desirable, is not an absolute requirement for parents in order to have their children baptized.

QUESTIONS FOR GROUP DISCUSSION

1. Why is Baptism so important?
2. What usually happens at a baptism?
3. What are the effects of Baptism?
4. How is faith related to Baptism?
5. What about all the people in the world who are not baptized? What happens to them?
6. What are baptismal promises?

QUESTIONS FOR PERSONAL REFLECTION

1. How has the sacrament of Baptism changed my life?
2. Do I live up to my baptismal promises?
3. Is my baptismal commitment a reality in my life?
4. Is my life a continual conversion to life in Christ?

BLESSING OF WATER

Father,
you give us grace through sacramental signs,
which tell us of the wonders of your unseen power.

In baptism we use your gift of water,
which you have made a rich symbol of the grace
you give us in this sacrament.

At the very dawn of creation
your Spirit breathed on the waters,
making them the wellspring of all holiness.

The waters of the great flood
you made a sign of the waters of baptism,
that make an end of sin
and a new beginning of goodness.

Through the waters of the Red Sea
you led Israel out of slavery,
to be an image of God's holy people,
set free from sin by baptism.

In the waters of the Jordan
your Son was baptized by John
and anointed with the Spirit.

Your Son willed that water and blood should flow from his side
as he hung upon the cross.

After his resurrection he told his disciples:
"Go out and teach all nations,
baptizing them in the name of the Father, and of the Son, and of the
    Holy Spirit."

Father,
look now with love upon your Church,
and unseal for it the fountain of baptism.

By the power of the Holy Spirit
give to this water the grace of your Son,
so that in the sacrament of baptism
all those whom you have created in your likeness
may be cleansed from sin
and rise to a new birth of innocence
by water and the Holy Spirit.

We ask you, Father, with your Son
to send the Holy Spirit upon the waters of this font.
May all who are buried with Christ in the death of baptism
rise also with him to newness of life.

We ask this through Christ our Lord.
Amen.

RITE OF BAPTISM
(RITE OF CHRISTIAN INITIATION OF ADULTS, 571)

CHAPTER 19

Confirmation

―――――

SCRIPTURE REFLECTION

When the time for Pentecost was fulfilled, they were all in one place together. And suddenly there came from the sky a noise like a strong driving wind, and it filled the entire house in which they were. Then there appeared to them tongues as of fire, which parted and came to rest on each one of them. And they were all filled with the holy Spirit and began to speak in different tongues, as the Spirit enabled them to proclaim.

Now there were devout Jews from every nation under heaven staying in Jerusalem. At this sound, they gathered in a large crowd, but they were confused because each one heard them speaking in his own language. They were astounded, and in amazement they asked, "Are not all these people who are speaking Galileans? Then how does each of us hear them in his own native language? We are Parthians, Medes, and Elamites, inhabitants of Mesopotamia, Judea and Cappadocia, Pontus and Asia, Phrygia and Pamphylia, Egypt and the districts of Libya near Cyrene, as well as travelers from Rome, both Jews and converts to Judaism, Cretans and Arabs, yet we hear them speaking in our own tongues of the mighty acts of God."

ACTS 2:1-11

INTRODUCTION

The sacrament of Confirmation, together with the sacraments of Baptism and Eucharist, comprise the sacraments of initiation. Through the celebration of these sacraments of initiation, a person enters full communion with the Church and is incorporated fully into the Body of Christ. A person who has celebrated the sacraments of initiation shares the responsibility to carry forward the mission of the Church in the world. This process is celebrated most beautifully for the adult in the baptismal catechumenate, which provides for the movement of the new believer from first hearing the Gospel (evangelization), to learning about the faith (catechumenate), to spiritual formation (illumination), and finally to a period of reflection on his or her new life in Christ (mystagogia). Usually the sacraments of initiation themselves are celebrated during the period of illumination, ideally at the Easter Vigil.

In particular, the sacrament of Confirmation strengthens a person's life in Christ that began at Baptism. In the New Testament, Confirmation was a unique encounter with the Holy Spirit, whose presence in the lives of the believers prepared them for their participation in the missionary work of the Church, which is to proclaim God's kingdom of justice and love.

STUDY QUESTIONS

1. Who may be confirmed?

"Every baptized person not yet confirmed can and should receive the sacrament of Confirmation (cf. CIC, can. 889 § 1). Since Baptism, Confirmation, and Eucharist form a unity, it follows that 'the faithful are obliged to receive this sacrament at the appropriate time' (CIC, can. 890), for without Confirmation and Eucharist, Baptism is certainly valid and efficacious, but Christian initiation remains incomplete" (CCC 1306). There are four requirements for a candidate for Confirmation who has attained the age of reason. He or she must profess the faith, be in the state of grace, have the intention of receiving the sacrament, and be prepared to assume the role of disciple and witness to Christ in the Church and in the world. In addition, it is recommended that the candidate receive the sacrament of Penance prior to Confirmation in order to be cleansed for the gift of the Holy Spirit. In those situations in which infants or very young children are confirmed, these requirements do not apply.

2. Is preparation for Confirmation necessary?

A suitable period of preparation should precede the actual celebration of the sacrament of Confirmation. "*Preparation* for Confirmation should aim at leading the Christian toward a more intimate union with Christ and a more lively familiarity with the Holy Spirit — his actions, his gifts, and his biddings — in order to be more capable of assuming the apostolic responsibilities of Christian life. To this end catechesis for Confirmation should strive to awaken a sense of belonging to the Church of Jesus Christ, the universal Church as well as the parish community. The latter bears special responsibility for the preparation of confirmands (cf. *OC* Introduction 3)" (CCC 1309).

3. Who is the minister of Confirmation?

Ordinarily, the bishop is the minister of Confirmation, but he may delegate certain priests to assist him. "Bishops are the successors of the apostles. They have received the fullness of the sacrament of Holy Orders. The administration of this sacrament by them demonstrates clearly that its effect is to unite those who receive it more closely to the Church, to her apostolic origins, and to her mission of bearing witness to Christ" (CCC 1313). When adult catechumens are baptized or persons baptized in other Christian communities are being received into full communion with the

Catholic Church, they may also be confirmed by the priest who is baptizing them or receiving them into full communion with the Catholic Church.

4. *How does the bishop confirm?*

"The essential rite of Confirmation is anointing the forehead of the baptized with sacred chrism … together with the laying on of the minister's hand and the words: … Be sealed with the Gift of the Holy Spirit" (CCC 1320).

5. *Who may act as a sponsor at Confirmation?*

"Candidates for Confirmation, as for Baptism, fittingly seek the spiritual help of a *sponsor*. To emphasize the unity of the two sacraments, it is appropriate that this be one of the baptismal godparents (cf. *OC* Introduction 5; 6; CIC, can. 893 §§ 1-2)" (CCC 1311). A practicing Catholic whose own faith is vibrant and growing can provide good example and spiritual support for the candidate for Confirmation.

6. *Does a Catholic have to be confirmed in order to be married in the Catholic Church?*

While every baptized Catholic should be confirmed, one does not have to be confirmed in order to receive the sacrament of Matrimony. For one who is not confirmed, seeking marriage in the Catholic Church provides a good opportunity to inquire about available assistance for the preparation and celebration of Confirmation.

QUESTIONS FOR GROUP DISCUSSION

1. How are the sacraments of initiation related to one another?
2. What is the Rite of Christian Initiation of Adults?
3. What is the significance of anointing in the sacrament of Confirmation?
4. How important is Confirmation in living a Christian life?

QUESTIONS FOR PERSONAL REFLECTION

1. Do I feel that I bear witness to Gospel values (love, peace, justice, mercy, compassion, reconciliation, etc.) in my daily life?
2. In concrete terms, how can I be of service to my family, friends, and community?
3. What does it mean to me to be "confirmed in my faith?"

PRAYER OF IMPOSITION

All-powerful God, Father of our Lord Jesus Christ,
by water and the Holy Spirit
you freed your sons and daughters from sin
and gave them new life.
Send your Holy Spirit upon them
to be their Helper and Guide.
Give them the spirit of wisdom and understanding,
the spirit of right judgment and courage,
the spirit of knowledge and reverence.
Fill them with the spirit of wonder and awe in your presence.
We ask this through Christ our Lord.
Amen.

RITE OF CONFIRMATION (N. 25)

CHAPTER 20

Eucharist

———

SCRIPTURE REFLECTION

Jesus said to them, "Amen, amen, I say to you, unless you eat the flesh of the Son of Man and drink his blood, you do not have life within you. Whoever eats my flesh and drinks my blood has eternal life, and I will raise him on the last day. For my flesh is true food, and my blood is true drink. Whoever eats my flesh and drinks my blood remains in me and I in him. Just as the living Father sent me and I have life because of the Father, so also the one who feeds on me will have life because of me. This is the bread that came down from heaven. Unlike your ancestors who ate and still died, whoever eats this bread will live forever."

JOHN 6:53-58

INTRODUCTION

Around the feast of the Jewish Passover, when Jesus gathered with his disciples to celebrate the traditional meal, they shared their last supper together and their first experience of the Eucharist. In this meal they remembered the covenant love through which they were related to God, and they began a new ritual that marked a new covenant, one in which Jesus himself was the expression of the Father's love.

Of all the sacraments, the Eucharist is the one that is celebrated most often. We will be nourished at the Table of the Lord by the Body and Blood of Christ many times throughout our lives. Our sharing in the Eucharist completes our process of incorporation into the Church and brings about a closer union with Christ and with all the members of the believing community. "As often as you eat this bread and drink the cup, you proclaim the death of the Lord until he comes" (1 Cor 11:26).

The Eucharist is the source and summit of the Church's life. Through the expression of its faith in the Eucharist, the Church deepens that faith. In the Eucharist Jesus is truly present as the saving events of the Paschal mystery are recalled and celebrated. He is truly present as well under the appearances of bread and wine that the people share in Holy Communion. Thus, the Eucharist is at once a memorial sacrifice, a sacrament, and a sacred meal.

The Eucharist is a memorial sacrifice because it memorializes the offering of a victim by a priest to God. Jesus is both the victim and the priest in the sacrifice of the Eucharist. He is the one offering the sacrifice in the person of the priest and the offering itself. He offered himself freely, suffering death on the cross for us. In the Eucharist the worshiping community enters into the sacrifice of Jesus, and the members pledge to incorporate themselves more fully into his mission.

The Eucharist is a sacrament because it is an effective sign of God's nourishing love, a symbol of unity, and a bond of charity. Even as the Eucharist reveals God's love, it causes God's love to be experienced and shared within the worshiping community. The sacrament of the Eucharist, Holy Communion, is indeed a sacred coming together, an intimate solidarity with God and one's sisters and brothers, a blessed sharing in God's gift of himself to all.

The Eucharist is a sacred meal because it brings about the nourishing effect it symbolizes. It is spiritual food. The Eucharist is the "bread of life" and the "cup of eternal salvation." The worshiping community shares the banquet of Jesus' love when they eat at the Table of the Lord. Just as ordinary food is converted into physical energy, the Eucharist nourishes the continual journey of the believer toward oneness with God. Sharing this sacred meal at once recalls the religious tradition of the Jewish Passover and foreshadows the eternal banquet to which God invites all.

STUDY QUESTIONS

1. Who may receive the Eucharist?

After having been baptized, any Catholic who is free from grave sin, who believes what the Church teaches about the Eucharist, and who has the proper disposition may receive Christ in the Eucharist. "Anyone who desires to receive Christ in Eucharistic communion must be in the state of grace. Anyone aware of having sinned mortally must not receive communion without having received absolution in the sacrament of penance" (CCC 1415).

2. Is Christ really present in the Eucharist?

"By the consecration the transubstantiation of the bread and wine into the Body and Blood of Christ is brought about. Under the consecrated species of bread and wine Christ himself, living and glorious, is present in a true, real, and substantial manner: his Body and his Blood, with his soul and his divinity (cf. Council of Trent: DS 1640; 1651)" (CCC 1413).

3. Who is the ordinary minister of Holy Communion?

"Only validly ordained priests can preside at the Eucharist and consecrate the bread and the wine so that they become the Body and Blood of the Lord" (CCC 1411). In the person of Christ, the priest leads the Christian assembly in the Eucharistic liturgy (the Mass) and is the ordinary minister of Holy Communion. Where there are not enough priests to distribute Holy Communion to the faithful, members of the laity may be properly trained and formally deputized to do so. They are called "extraordinary ministers of Holy Communion."

4. *Is there still a fast before a person can receive Holy Communion?*
Yes. Appropriate preparation for the reception of Holy Communion is made when the person does not eat or drink anything except water or medicine for one hour before receiving the Eucharist. A sick or aged person is not bound by this regulation. "To prepare for worthy reception of this sacrament, the faithful should observe the fast required in their Church (cf. CIC, can. 919). Bodily demeanor (gestures, clothing) ought to convey the respect, solemnity, and joy of this moment when Christ becomes our guest" (CCC 1387).

5. *How does a person receive Holy Communion?*
Ordinarily, Holy Communion is received on the tongue. Subject to the local bishop's decision, however, Holy Communion may also be received in the hand. The minister raises the host and says, "The Body of Christ." Making a slight bow of the head to acknowledge Christ's presence in the sacred species, the communicant responds by saying, "Amen." In addition, the Eucharist may be offered under both kinds, which means that the communicant receives the host and then is invited to drink from a cup containing the Blood of Christ. In this case the minister presents the cup to the communicant and says, "The Blood of Christ." The communicant again responds by bowing and saying, "Amen."

6. *Can fellow Christians who are not Catholics receive Holy Communion?*
The ecumenical guidelines approved by the leaders of both the Catholic Church and other Christian churches state that a Christian who is not a Catholic should not receive Holy Communion in a Catholic Church. Intercommunion among Christians is the goal for which the churches are striving, but it

should not be used as a way to achieve Christian unity. Only when a grave necessity arises may Catholic ministers give the sacrament of the Eucharist to other Christians not in full communion with the Catholic Church. In these situations of grave necessity, in order for a Christian who is not a Catholic to receive Holy Communion in a Catholic Church, he or she must have a faith in the sacrament that conforms to the Catholic Church, experience a serious spiritual need for the sacrament, be unable for a prolonged period of time to receive Communion in his or her own Church, ask for the sacrament of his or her own accord, and have the proper disposition. Members of other religions, such as Jews, Muslims, Buddhists, etc., do not believe in Christ. While they can join Catholics in praying for the unity of all mankind, they should not receive the Body and Blood of Christ in Holy Communion.

7. *How often should a person receive Holy Communion?*

"The Church warmly recommends that the faithful receive Holy Communion when they participate in the celebration of the Eucharist; she obliges them to do so at least once a year" (CCC 1417). Holy Communion should be received each time a properly disposed Catholic participates in the Mass. Receiving the Eucharist is a sign of full communion with the life of the Church, and that sign ideally should be demonstrated at each celebration of the Eucharist. A person may receive Holy Communion twice in one day if that person participates in two different Eucharistic liturgies. The Church requires all Catholics "to receive the Eucharist at least once a year, if possible during the Easter season (cf. *OE* 15; CIC, can. 920)" (CCC 1389).

QUESTIONS FOR GROUP DISCUSSION

1. What is the significance of the Passover meal?
2. How is the Eucharist a sacrifice?

3. What does it mean for us to participate in the Eucharist?

4. How is Christ really present in the Eucharist?

5. What is our role in celebrating the Eucharist?

6. How does the Eucharist affect our daily lives?

7. What does it mean to receive Holy Communion "under both kinds"?

8. Why are lay people permitted to distribute Holy Communion?

QUESTIONS FOR PERSONAL REFLECTION

1. Is the Eucharist the center of my Christian life?

2. When I receive the Eucharist, is it a pledge for me to work in my own way for God's Kingdom of justice and love?

3. Do I grow in my understanding and appreciation of the Eucharist as I grow older in years?

4. Is the celebration of the Eucharist an experience of prayer for me?

ANIMA CHRISTI

Soul of Christ, sanctify me.

Body of Christ, save me.

Blood of Christ, inebriate me.

Water from the side of Christ, wash me.

Passion of Christ, strengthen me.

O good Jesus, hear me.

Within your wounds hide me.

Never permit me to be separated from you.

From the wicked enemy defend me.

At the hour of my death call me,

And bid me come to you;

That with your saints I may praise you,

For ever and ever.

Amen.

CHAPTER 21

Penance and Reconciliation

———

SCRIPTURE REFLECTION

On the evening of that first day of the week, when the doors were locked, where the disciples were, for fear of the Jews, Jesus came and stood in their midst and said to them, "Peace be with you." When he had said this, he showed them his hands and his side. The disciples rejoiced when they saw the Lord. [Jesus] said to them again, "Peace be with you. As the Father has sent me, so I send you." And when he had said this, he breathed on them and said to them, "Receive the holy Spirit. Whose sins you forgive are forgiven them, and whose sins you retain are retained."

JOHN 20:19-23

INTRODUCTION

In the course of our journey toward the Kingdom of God, at times we turn away from our lifetime goal to be one with him for all eternity. Often we fail in loving God and our neighbors, and we sin. The Church responds to the situation of personal sin with a sign of Christ's forgiveness and healing, the sacrament of Penance and Reconciliation. Through our celebration of the sacrament of Penance and Reconciliation, our loving relationship with God and the Church is restored. In people who acknowledge their sinfulness, who express sorrow in their own hearts, and who seek to change and make a fresh start, the Holy Spirit has already begun the process of sacramental forgiveness.

A person may receive the sacrament of Penance and Reconciliation in three ways: first, through individual confession; second, in a communal penance service that includes individual confessions; and third, in a communal penance service that includes general absolution. Individual confession with absolution is the ordinary way Catholics receive the sacrament of Penance and Reconciliation. A communal penance service emphasizes our intimate connection to a community of believers and our need to be reconciled with both God and the community. Ordinarily, the communal service includes prayers, Scripture readings, hymns, a homily, an examination of conscience, and the opportunity for individual confession and absolution. Only in a case of grave necessity, however, may general absolution be validly given at a communal penance service.

> Grave necessity of this sort can arise when there is imminent danger of death without sufficient time for the priest or priests to hear each penitent's confession. Grave necessity can also exist when, given the number of penitents, there are not enough confessors to hear individual confessions properly in a reasonable time, so that the penitents through no fault of their own would be deprived of sacramental grace or Holy Communion for a long time. In this case, for the absolution to be valid the faithful must have the intention of individually confessing their grave sins in the time required (cf. CIC, can. 962 § 1). The diocesan bishop is the judge of whether or not the conditions required for general absolution exist (cf. CIC, can. 961 § 2). A large gathering of the faithful on the occasion of major feasts or pilgrimages does not constitute a grave necessity (cf. CIC, can. 961 § 1) [CCC 1483].

Those who receive general absolution within a communal penance service must confess serious sins individually as soon as possible so that the confessor may impose a particular penance and give proper personal direction.

STUDY QUESTIONS

1. Who may receive the sacrament of Penance and Reconciliation?

"To return to communion with God after having lost it through sin is a process born of the grace of God who is rich in mercy and solicitous for the salvation of men. One must ask for this precious gift for oneself and for others" (CCC 1489). Any baptized Catholic who has sorrow for sin and the intention to avoid sin in the future may receive the sacrament of Penance and Reconciliation.

2. In general, what does the sacrament of Penance and Reconciliation involve?

In general, the sacrament of Penance and Reconciliation is a personal encounter with Christ who reaches out in healing mercy and forgiveness to the repentant sinner. The minister of the sacrament, the priest, acts in the person of Christ and represents the Church as he stands with the penitent under the healing grace of the sacrament. The penitent admits sin, expresses sorrow, accepts a penance, and resolves to try to avoid sin in the future. The Second Vatican Council states, "Those who approach the sacrament of Penance obtain pardon from God's mercy for the offense committed against him, and are, at the same time, reconciled with the Church which they have wounded by their sins and which by charity, by example, and by prayer labors for their conversion" (*Dogmatic Constitution on the Church*, 11)

3. How does one celebrate the sacrament of Penance and Reconciliation?

"Like all the sacraments, Penance is a liturgical action. The elements of the celebration are ordinarily these: a greeting and blessing from the priest, reading the word of God to illuminate the conscience and elicit contrition, and an exhortation to repentance; the confession, which acknowledges sins and makes them known to the priest; the imposition and acceptance of a penance; the priest's absolution; a prayer of thanksgiving and praise and dismissal with the blessing of the priest" (CCC 1480).

The process begins with a private examination of one's conscience or a review of one's immediate past. Then the penitent enters the confessional or reconciliation room and begins by making the sign of the cross. The penitent tells the priest how long it has been since the last confession, or perhaps that this is his or her first confession. The priest may welcome the penitent and choose to read a brief passage from Sacred Scripture. The penitent then confesses his or her sins. The priest may have a word of advice or a question of clarification, after which he will assign a penance and invite the penitent to say a prayer of sorrow. The priest then extends his hand over the penitent and proclaims the words of absolution. The priest then urges the penitent to go in peace.

4. What is the basic role of the confessor in the sacrament of Penance and Reconciliation?

When he celebrates the sacrament of Penance and Reconciliation, the priest is a sign and instrument of God's merciful love for the sinner. He acts in the person of Christ, the divine physician of our souls, as the Good Shepherd who seeks out the one who was lost, the good Samaritan who binds up the wounds of the fallen, and the father of the prodigal son who welcomes him at his return home. The priest is to be a just and compassionate judge. "The confessor is not the master of God's forgiveness, but its servant. The minister of this sacrament should unite himself to the intention and charity of Christ (cf. *PO* 13). He should have a proven knowledge of

Christian behavior, experience of human affairs, respect and sensitivity toward the one who has fallen; he must love the truth, be faithful to the Magisterium of the Church, and lead the penitent with patience toward healing and full maturity. He must pray and do penance for his penitent, entrusting him to the Lord's mercy" (CCC 1466).

5. *What is a penance?*

"The confessor proposes the performance of certain acts of 'satisfaction' or 'penance' to be performed by the penitent in order to repair the harm caused by sin and to re-establish habits befitting a disciple of Christ" (CCC 1494). The penance that the priest assigns the penitent in the sacrament of Penance and Reconciliation usually takes the form of a prayer or a good work that is said or done outside the confessional or reconciliation room. Performing the penance does not make up for one's sin, but rather shows the intention of the penitent to avoid sin in the future.

6. *What are the words of absolution?*

These are the words the priest proclaims over the penitent that confer the grace of the sacrament. They are: "God the Father of mercies, through the death and resurrection of his Son has reconciled the world to himself and sent the Holy Spirit among us for the forgiveness of sins; through the ministry of the Church may God give you pardon and peace, and I absolve you from your sins in the name of the Father, and of the Son, and of the Holy Spirit." And the penitent responds, "Amen" (*Rite of Penance*, 46).

7. *When should a person celebrate the sacrament of Penance and Reconciliation?*

The Christian life is a continual process of conversion to Christ, and so a person should celebrate the sacrament of Penance and Reconciliation frequently. "One who desires to obtain reconciliation with God and with the Church, must confess to a priest all the unconfessed grave sins he remembers after having carefully examined his conscience. The confession of venial faults, without being necessary in itself, is nevertheless strongly recommended by the Church" (CCC 1493). A good personal discipline would be to celebrate the sacrament of Penance and Reconciliation once a month, but minimally twice yearly, once during Advent, the time before Christmas, and once during Lent, the time before Easter. If one has committed mortal sin, one must receive the sacrament of Penance and Reconciliation once a year — prior to receiving the Eucharist during the Easter season.

8. *When must a person celebrate the sacrament of Penance and Reconciliation?*

Grave or mortal sin severs a person's relationship with God and the Church. A person must celebrate the sacrament of Penance and Reconciliation when he or she has committed mortal sin, in order to restore those relationships. "Individual and integral confession of grave sins followed by absolution remains the only ordinary means of reconciliation with God and with the Church" (CCC 1497).

9. *Can a person go to Holy Communion if that person has been involved in grave or mortal sin?*

"Sin is before all else an offense against God, a rupture of communion with him. At the same time it damages communion with the Church" (CCC 1440). Grave or mortal sin severs the person's relationship with God and the Church. The Eucharist, or Holy Communion, is the preeminent sign of unity with God and with the Body of Christ, the Church. A person should not receive Holy Communion, the sign of unity with God and the Church, when he or she has committed mortal sin, which is fundamental disunity.

10. *What is an act of perfect contrition?*

"When it arises from a love by which God is loved above all else, contrition is called 'perfect' (contrition of charity). Such contrition remits venial sins; it also obtains forgiveness of mortal sins if it includes the firm resolution to have recourse to sacramental confession as soon as possible (cf. Council of Trent [1551]: DS 1677)" (CCC 1452).

QUESTIONS FOR GROUP DISCUSSION

1. Why is the sacrament of Penance and Reconciliation a valuable experience for us?
2. Is reconciliation with the Church as important as reconciliation with the Lord?
3. Why does the Church require individual confession of mortal sins to a priest?
4. Are there other ways for sin to be forgiven?
5. How can we identify sin in our lives?

QUESTIONS FOR PERSONAL REFLECTION

1. Is it hard for me to acknowledge that I am a sinner in need of forgiveness?
2. Do I seem to repeat the same sins over and over again?
3. Do I see the value in individual confession?
4. I know that God forgives me, but can I really forgive myself?

PRAYER OF REPENTANCE

LORD, hear my prayer;
in your faithfulness listen to my pleading;
answer me in your justice.
Do not enter into judgment with your servant;
before you no living being can be just.
The enemy has pursued me;
they have crushed my life to the ground.
They have left me in darkness
like those long dead.
My spirit is faint within me;
my heart is dismayed.
I remember the days of old;
I ponder all your deeds;
the works of your hands I recall.
I stretch out my hands to you;
I thirst for you like a parched land.
Hasten to answer me, LORD;
for my spirit fails me.
Do not hide your face from me,
lest I become like those descending to the pit.
At dawn let me hear of your kindness,
for in you I trust.
Show me the path I should walk,
for to you I entrust my life.
Rescue me, LORD, from my foes,
for in you I hope.
Teach me to do your will,
for you are my God.

May your kind spirit guide me
   on ground that is level.
For your name's sake, LORD, give me life;
   in your justice lead me out of distress.
In your kindness put an end to my foes;
   destroy all who attack me,
   for I am your servant.

PSALM 143:1-12

CHAPTER 22
Anointing of the Sick

―――

SCRIPTURE REFLECTION

Is anyone among you sick? He should summon the presbyters of the church, and they should pray over him and anoint [him] with oil in the name of the Lord, and the prayer of faith will save the sick person, and the Lord will raise him up. If he has committed any sins, he will be forgiven.

Therefore, confess your sins to one another and pray for one another, that you may be healed.

JAMES 5:14-16

INTRODUCTION

From the earliest apostolic times, the religious leaders of the people have anointed and prayed over the sick for the purpose of spiritual assistance. The purpose of the anointing is to give Christ's own comfort and strength to the person who is face-to-face with suffering and mortality. Serious illness causes a person to confront personal humanness, frailty, and dependence. For the Christian, that confrontation is not faced alone, but rather with the personal company of the Lord as well as the consolation of the believing community, the Church. The sacrament of the Anointing of the Sick is not the sacrament of the dying; the Eucharist, or viaticum, is the sacrament of the dying. The sacrament of the Anointing of the Sick seeks to uplift the one suffering, join the one suffering to the sufferings of Jesus, forgive sin, and encourage physical health. The spiritual effects of illness and the meaning of human suffering are primary considerations as the Church seeks to ease the pain of those who are sick.

While the sacrament of the Anointing of the Sick is often administered individually to the sick person, sometimes in the presence of a few family members, its most appropriate celebration is in a communal setting where the whole community can have the benefit of experiencing the identification of the Lord's suffering with the suffering of its sick members. The Church places the sick in the Lord's care and gathers in prayerful support around those who are participating in Christ's suffering.

STUDY QUESTIONS

1. *Who may receive the sacrament of the Anointing of the Sick?*

   Any baptized Catholic who is seriously ill due to sickness or advancing age may receive the sacrament of the Anointing of the Sick. Reception of the sacrament of the Anointing of the Sick should not be delayed until the person is at the point of death. "The proper time for receiving this holy anointing has certainly arrived when the believer begins to be in danger of death because of illness or old age" (CCC 1528).

2. *How often may the sacrament be received?*

   The sacrament of the Anointing of the Sick demonstrates the care of Christ and his Church for the person threatened with illness, an illness that may have several stages. "Each time a Christian falls seriously ill, he may receive the Anointing of the Sick, and also when, after he has received it, the illness worsens" (CCC 1529). So the sacrament of the Anointing of the Sick can be received several times throughout one's lifetime.

3. *Who is the minister of the sacrament of the Anointing of the Sick?*
Only bishops and priests may administer the sacrament of the Anointing of the Sick. "It is the duty of pastors to instruct the faithful on the benefits of this sacrament. The faithful should encourage the sick to call for a priest to receive this sacrament. The sick should prepare themselves to receive it with good dispositions, assisted by their pastor and the whole ecclesial community, which is invited to surround the sick in a special way through their prayers and fraternal attention" (CCC 1516).

4. *Is the sacrament of the Anointing of the Sick for people who are at the point of death and is therefore commonly referred to as the "last" sacrament or the "last rites?"*
The sacrament of the Anointing of the Sick is not reserved for those who are at the point of death. The sacrament of the dying, the last sacrament, is properly the Eucharist. In this situation the Eucharist is called "viaticum," or "May the Lord go with you." It is the spiritual food for one's passing over to the Father. "It is the seed of eternal life and the power of resurrection" (CCC 1524). The reception of the Holy Eucharist as viaticum together with Penance and Anointing of the Sick constitute the sacraments that complete our pilgrimage on earth.

5. *How is the sacrament of the Anointing of the Sick administered?*
"Like all the sacraments the Anointing of the Sick is a liturgical and communal celebration (cf. *SC* 27), whether it takes place in the family home, a hospital or church, for a single sick person or a whole group of sick persons. It is very fitting to celebrate it within the Eucharist, the memorial of the Lord's Passover" (CCC 1517). The priest lays his hands on the sick, prays over them in the faith of the Church, then anoints them with oil ordinarily blessed by the bishop. The priest traces the sign of the cross with the blessed oil

on the forehead of the sick person, saying, "Through this holy anointing, may the Lord in his love and mercy help you with the grace of the Holy Spirit." Then, anointing the palms of the hands in the same way, the priest says: "May the Lord who frees you from sin save you and raise you up" (*Pastoral Care of the Sick*, 25).

QUESTIONS FOR GROUP DISCUSSION

1. What is the meaning of suffering?
2. Can an individual's illness affect the Church?
3. How should Catholics view death?
4. In what sense does the sacrament of the Anointing of the Sick accomplish healing in the sick person?
5. What are the "last rites" of the Church?

QUESTIONS FOR PERSONAL REFLECTION

1. What is my personal attitude toward sickness?
2. Do I see the relationship between suffering and salvation?
3. What is my experience of sickness, suffering, and death?
4. Do I see any connection between my suffering and the suffering of the Lord?

PRAYER AFTER ANOINTING

Lord, Jesus Christ,
you chose to share in our human nature,
to redeem all people, and to heal the sick.

Look with compassion upon your servant N.,
whom we have anointed in your name with this holy oil
for the healing of his/her body and spirit.

Support him/her with your power,
comfort him/her with your protection,
and give him/her the strength to fight against evil.

Since you have given him/her a share in your own passion,
help him/her to find hope in suffering,
for you are Lord for ever and ever.
Amen.

RITE OF ANOINTING
(PASTORAL CARE OF THE SICK, 125)

CHAPTER 23
Holy Orders

═══

SCRIPTURE REFLECTION

Every high priest is taken from among men and made their representative before God, to offer gifts and sacrifices for sins. He is able to deal patiently with the ignorant and erring, for he himself is beset by weakness and so, for this reason, must make sin offerings for himself as well as for the people. No one takes this honor upon himself but only when called by God, just as Aaron was. In the same way, it was not Christ who glorified himself in becoming high priest, but rather the one who said to him:

"You are my son;
this day I have begotten you."

HEBREWS 5:1-5

INTRODUCTION

Jesus sent his apostles into the world to preach the Kingdom of God, to exhort people to conversion, to cast out devils, to heal the sick (Mk 6:7-13), to celebrate his memory in the Eucharist (1 Cor 11:23-26), and to forgive sins (Jn 20:21-23). The apostles, in turn, handed on Christ's commission of apostolic preaching and authority, as a permanent office in the Church, to their successors, the bishops, through the laying on of hands. This sacrament of apostolic authority will continue to be exercised in the Church until the end of time.

While the whole Church is a priestly people, those who are called to Holy Orders participate in Christ's mission by serving the common priesthood of the faithful. They serve in the name and person of Jesus Christ, the Head of his Body, the Church. They exercise their service for the People of God by teaching, divine worship, and pastoral governance. Since the foundation of the Church by Christ, the ordained ministry has included three degrees: bishops, priests, and deacons. These ministries conferred by the ordination are essential elements in the organizational structure of the Church. As successors to the apostles, bishops receive the fullness of the sacrament of Holy Orders and share in the apostolic responsibility and mission of the whole Church under the authority of the Pope. Priests are the principle co-workers of the bishops. They form a presbyterium around him and with him bear the responsibility for the local Church. Sacramental ordination confers on deacons important functions, under the authority of their bishop, in the ministry of the Word, divine worship, pastoral governance, and charity.

STUDY QUESTIONS

1. *Who may receive the sacrament of Holy Orders?*

A baptized male Catholic of excellent character and appropriate age and level of learning, who intends to devote his life to the ministerial priesthood and who is called by the local bishop may receive the sacrament of Holy Orders. "The Church confers the sacrament of Holy Orders only on baptized men (*viri*), whose suitability for the exercise of the ministry has been duly recognized. Church authority alone has the responsibility and right to call someone to receive the sacrament of Holy Orders" (CCC 1598).

Ordinarily, that vocation is discovered and tested over a period of years in specialized training for the ordained ministry.

2. Who is the minister of the sacrament of Holy Orders?

"Since the sacrament of Holy Orders is the sacrament of the apostolic ministry, it is for the bishops as the successors of the apostles to hand on the 'gift of the Spirit' (*LG* 21 § 2), the 'apostolic line' (*LG* 20). Validly ordained bishops, i.e., those who are in the line of apostolic succession, validly confer the three degrees of the sacrament of Holy Orders (cf. DS 794 and cf. DS 802; CIC, can. 1012; CCEO, can. 744; 747)" (CCC 1576).

3. How is the sacrament of Holy Orders administered?

"The sacrament of Holy Orders is conferred by the laying on of hands followed by a solemn prayer of consecration asking God to grant the ordinand the graces of the Holy Spirit required for his ministry. Ordination imprints an indelible sacramental character" (CCC 1597). The grace of the sacrament of Holy Orders configures the ordinand to Christ so that he may act in the person of Christ for the service of the Church. One cannot receive the sacrament of Holy Orders more than once, nor can it be conferred temporarily.

4. Can priests marry?

In the Eastern Church, married men may become priests. In the Western Church, only men who are willing to lead celibate lives can become priests. The Church has never permitted priests to marry after their ordination. The discipline of the Church requires celibacy, the free choice not to marry, in the ordained priesthood. "All the ordained ministers of the Latin Church, with the exception of permanent deacons, are normally chosen from among men of faith who live a celibate life and who intend to remain celibate 'for the sake of the kingdom of heaven' (Mt 19:12). Called to consecrate themselves with undivided heart to the Lord and to 'the affairs of the Lord' (1 Cor 7:32), they give themselves entirely to God and to men. Celibacy is a sign of this new life to the service of which the Church's minister is consecrated; accepted with a joyous heart celibacy radiantly proclaims the Reign of God (cf. *PO* 16)" (CCC 1579).

5. Can women be priests?

"No one has a *right* to receive the sacrament of Holy Orders. Indeed no one claims this office for himself; he is called to it by God (cf. Heb 5:4). Anyone who thinks he recognizes the signs of God's call to the ordained ministry must humbly submit his desire to the authority of the Church, who has the responsibility and right to call someone to receive orders. Like every grace this sacrament can be *received* only as an unmerited gift" (CCC 1578).

All the baptized are called to participate in the common priesthood of the faithful, which is a genuine sharing in the priesthood of Christ. Women are excluded only from the ordained ministry. In fact, they exercise ministry in education, in liturgy, in pastoral care, and in all areas of Church life. The Church does not believe that women are inferior to men. The Church teaches that Christ does not call women to the ministerial priesthood and consequently the Church is not free to ordain women to the priesthood. Pope John Paul II declared that "the Church has no authority whatsoever to confer priestly ordination on women and that this judgment is to be definitively held by all the Christian faithful" (*Apostolic Letter on Reserving Priestly Ordination to Men Alone*, n. 4).

6. Can a priest leave the priesthood?

A priest may petition the Pope to be released from his orders and may be permitted to leave the active priesthood, but one who is ordained a priest remains a priest forever.

It is true that someone validly ordained can, for grave reasons, be discharged from the obligations and functions linked to ordination, or can be forbidden to exercise them; but he cannot become a layman again in the strict sense (cf. CIC, cann. 290-293; 1336 § 1 3°, 5°; 1338 § 2; Council of Trent: DS 1774), because the character imprinted by ordination is for ever.

The vocation and mission received on the day of his ordination mark him permanently [CCC 1583].

QUESTIONS FOR GROUP DISCUSSION

1. In what sense is Jesus a priest?
2. How can a person tell he is being called to the priesthood?
3. What is the role of the deacon in the Church?
4. What is the role of the bishop in the Church?
5. Why can't priests marry?
6. Why can't women be priests?
7. What's the difference between diocesan and religious-order priests?
8. Why are we all called to holiness?

QUESTIONS FOR PERSONAL REFLECTION

1. What do I think of priests in general?
2. Do I know any priests personally?
3. Would I want my son to be a priest?
4. What would the Church do without priests?

Prayer of Consecration

Come to our help,
Lord, holy Father, almighty and eternal God;
you are the source of every honor and dignity,
of all progress and stability.
You watch over the growing family of man
by your gift of wisdom and your pattern of order.
When you had appointed high priests to rule your people,
you chose other men next to them in rank and dignity
to be with them and help them in their task;
and so there grew up
the ranks of priests and the offices of levites,
established by sacred rites.

In the desert
you extended the spirit of Moses to seventy wise men
who helped him to rule the great company of his people.
You shared among the sons of Aaron
the fullness of their father's power,
to provide worthy priests in sufficient number
for the increasing rites of sacrifice and worship.
With the same loving care
you gave companions to your Son's apostles
to help in teaching the faith:
they preached the Gospel to the whole world.

Lord, grant also to us such fellow workers,
for we are weak and our need is greater.

Almighty Father,
grant to these servants of yours
the dignity of the priesthood.
Renew within them the Spirit of holiness.
As co-workers with the order of bishops
may they be faithful to their ministry
that they receive from you, Lord God,
and be to others a model of right conduct.

May they be faithful in working with the order of bishops,
so that the words of the Gospel may reach the ends of the earth,
and the family of nations,
made one in Christ,
may become God's one, holy people.

We ask this through our Lord Jesus Christ, your Son,
who lives and reigns with you and the Holy Spirit,
one God, for ever and ever.
Amen.

RITE OF ORDINATION
(ORDINATION OF DEACONS, PRIESTS, AND BISHOPS, 26)

CHAPTER 24
Matrimony

═══

SCRIPTURE REFLECTION

The LORD God said: "It is not good for the man to be alone. I will make a suitable partner for him."

... So the LORD God cast a deep sleep on the man, and while he was asleep, he took out one of his ribs and closed up its place with flesh. The LORD God then built up into a woman the rib that he had taken from the man. When he brought her to the man, the man said:

> "This one, at last, is bone of
>> my bones
> and flesh of my flesh;
> This one shall be called 'woman,'
>> for out of 'her man' this one has been taken."

That is why a man leaves his father and mother and clings to his wife, and the two of them become one body.

GENESIS 2:18, 21-24

INTRODUCTION

God is the author of marriage. Christian marriage is an encounter with Christ. In this encounter, human love and God's love cooperate to establish an enduring, faithful, and fruitful covenant.

Throughout the pages of Scripture, the predominant symbol of God's relationship to his people is the covenant. In a very real sense, our relationship to God is a marriage. We are the beloved of the Lord, just as the bride is the beloved of the groom. This is why the Church is sometimes referred to as the Bride of Christ. Permanence, fidelity, and sanctity describe both God's covenant with his people and the marriage of woman and man. The love of husband and wife is modeled after Christ's selfless love for the Church (Eph 5:22-33).

While there are always difficult times in any relationship, the permanent commitment of Christian marriage is intended for the stability of the couple, the family, and society in general. The couple's promise of mutual fidelity ensures an exclusive kind of love that is meant to be shared only between the man and the woman. By its very nature the marital relationship of the couple is sacred. Their bond is strengthened by the grace of Christ and by the support of the community of believers. This kind of marriage reflects the intensity of God's love for his people.

Ordinarily, serious preparation for Christian marriage is both desired by the couple and expected by the Church parish. The Church, through the local parish, seeks to assist the couple in their preparation for marriage through discussion, instruction, and prayer, so that a happy and successful marriage may be celebrated and lived for the good of the spouses, the good of the Church, and the good of society in general.

STUDY QUESTIONS

1. Is marriage a sacrament?

"The marriage covenant, by which a man and a woman form with each other an intimate communion of life and love, has been founded and endowed with its own special laws by the Creator. By its very nature it is ordered to the good of the couple, as well as to the generation and education of children. Christ the Lord raised marriage between the baptized to the dignity of a sacrament (cf. CIC, can. 1055 § 1; cf. *GS* 48 § 1)" (CCC 1660). The marriage of two baptized persons is the sacrament by which Christ joins a Christian man and woman in a permanent, faithful, and life-giving union.

2. *Who may celebrate the sacrament of Matrimony?*

Any baptized Catholic who is free to marry has a right to be married in the Catholic Church. Two Catholics who are free to contract marriage and freely express their consent, or a Catholic and a non-Catholic who are free to marry and freely express their consent, and who have obtained the appropriate permission, may celebrate the sacrament of Matrimony.

3. *How is the sacrament of Matrimony celebrated?*

The sacrament of Matrimony usually takes place in a Catholic Church before a priest and two witnesses, but, with permission, it can be celebrated in a non-Catholic setting before a non-Catholic minister and two witnesses. "Since marriage establishes the couple in a public state of life in the Church, it is fitting that its celebration be public, in the framework of a liturgical celebration, before the priest (or a witness authorized by the Church), the witnesses, and the assembly of the faithful" (CCC 1663). It is most fitting that the sacrament of Matrimony be celebrated at a Eucharistic liturgy and that the bride and groom prepare themselves for their marriage and to receive Holy Communion at their wedding Mass by receiving the sacrament of Penance.

4. *What does it mean "to be free" to marry?*

" 'To be free' means: not being under constraint; not impeded by any natural or ecclesiastical law" (CCC 1625). Freedom to marry refers to the absence of any impediments or hindrances, such as not having reached the legal age, not being psychologically mature, already being in a valid marriage, being forced, marrying on account of fear, or being impotent.

5. *What is a sacramental marriage?*

" 'From a valid marriage arises *a bond* between the spouses which by its very nature is perpetual and exclusive; furthermore, in a Christian marriage the spouses are strengthened and, as it were, consecrated for the duties and the dignity of their state *by a special sacrament*' (cf. CIC, can. 1134)" (CCC 1638). A sacramental marriage begins when two Catholics or a Catholic and a non-Catholic who are free to marry give true matrimonial consent before a priest or properly dispensed minister and two witnesses. The lifelong, loving commitment of the couple continues throughout a sacramental marriage. A sacramental marriage is an intimate encounter with Christ, which confers the grace necessary for the couple to live a permanent, faithful, and productive commitment.

6. *Can non-Catholics be witnesses at Catholic marriages?*

A non-Catholic Christian, such as a member of an Orthodox Church or another Christian Church, may act as one of the two official witnesses at a Catholic marriage. Catholics can be witnesses at properly celebrated marriages of non-Catholics.

7. *Who is the minister of the sacrament of Matrimony?*

"According to the Latin tradition, the spouses, as ministers of Christ's grace mutually confer upon each other the sacrament of Matrimony by expressing their consent before the Church" (CCC 1623). The couple themselves, therefore, are the ministers of the sacrament of Matrimony. As they bestow their mutual consent freely upon each other, the grace of the sacrament is conferred upon them. The priest, or in some cases the deacon, acts as the official witness of the Church and bestows the Church's blessing, but the couple are the ministers of the sacrament.

8. Does a sacramental marriage ever end?

A valid sacramental marriage ends with the death of one's spouse.

9. Can a sacramental marriage ever be dissolved?

"*The marriage bond* has been established by God himself in such a way that a marriage concluded and consummated between baptized persons can never be dissolved. This bond, which results from the free human act of the spouses and their consummation of the marriage, is a reality, henceforth irrevocable, and gives rise to a covenant guaranteed by God's fidelity. The Church does not have the power to contravene this disposition of divine wisdom (cf. CIC, can. 1141)" (CCC 1640). The bond of a valid sacramental marriage endures until the death of one of the spouses.

10. Does the Church grant divorces?

The Church does not grant divorces or permit remarriage for validly married Catholics. "Yet there are some situations in which living together becomes practically impossible for a variety of reasons. In such cases the Church permits the physical *separation* of the couple and their living apart. The spouses do not cease to be husband and wife before God and so are not free to contract a new union. In this difficult situation, the best solution would be, if possible, reconciliation. The Christian community is called to help these persons live out their situation in a Christian manner and in fidelity to their marriage bond which remains indissoluble (cf. *FC* 83; CIC, cann. 1151-1155)" (CCC 1649).

11. What is an annulment?

An annulment or decree of nullity is the Church's official acknowledgment that an apparent marriage was never a sacramental marriage. If, for example, one or both of the partners was incapable of giving free consent or did not intend a permanent, faithful, and life-giving union, the Church, after careful investigation by proper authority, could grant an annulment. "The Church, after an examination of the situation by the competent ecclesiastical tribunal, can declare the nullity of a marriage, i.e., that the marriage never existed (cf. CIC, cann. 1095-1107). In this case the contracting parties are free to marry, provided the natural obligations of a previous union are discharged (cf. CIC, can. 1071)" (CCC 1629).

12. Is a Church annulment the same as a divorce?

A divorce is the result of a civil process that severs the bond of a civil marriage and sees to child support, custody, alimony, and property settlement. An annulment is a Church declaration that the marriage in question was not a sacramental one.

13. Does the Church permit divorce?

The Church permits married partners to separate only for serious reasons. Upon the advice of a competent authority, they may also seek to secure a civil divorce to protect their legal rights. A sacramental marriage still endures, however, and the spouses are not permitted to remarry in the Church unless an annulment can be obtained. Each diocese has a matrimonial tribunal, which hears and judges marriage cases.

14. How is an annulment obtained?

If one of the partners did not give consent freely or was incapable of giving consent freely to the marriage, or if one of the partners did not intend a permanent bond of faithful love open to the procreation of children, it is possible that no sacramental marriage was established. In these cases, one of the partners should talk the matter over with a parish minister, who will help bring the marriage in question before the competent matrimonial tribunal.

15. Are divorced people excommunicated from the Church?

No. Divorced people may participate fully in the life of the Church, including the reception of the Eucharist.

16. *If a divorced person obtains an annulment, can he or she remarry in the Catholic Church?*

The annulment declares that the marriage in question was never a binding sacramental one. That doesn't mean it was sinful but simply that it was irregular in some way in the judgment of the competent matrimonial tribunal. Receiving an annulment, therefore, frees the persons involved to enter into a sacramental marriage in the Catholic Church as long as the natural obligations of the previous marriage, such as provision for children of the union, are properly met.

17. *How can an annulment be granted if there were children of the marriage?*

The annulment does not depend on any development after the marriage, but rather judges that from the beginning no sacramental marriage ever existed. There was a legal or civil marriage but not a sacramental marriage.

18. *Does that mean that children of a marriage that is later annulled by the Church are illegitimate?*

No. Children born of a legal marriage that has subsequently been found by the Church not to be a valid sacramental marriage are legitimate. A Church annulment of a marriage does not affect the legal status of the prior marriage and therefore does not affect the legitimacy of children born of the marriage.

QUESTIONS FOR GROUP DISCUSSION

1. Why is the Church so strict on divorce and remarriage?
2. How does the Church view marriages of non-Catholics?
3. What are the grounds for annulment?
4. What is a mixed marriage?
5. What is the Pauline Privilege?
6. How does one begin the annulment process?
7. What does the Church teach about premarital sex, extramarital sex, cohabitation, and family planning?

QUESTIONS FOR PERSONAL REFLECTION

1. Can I love another permanently and faithfully?
2. Can I be loved by another permanently and faithfully?
3. How well do I communicate? Listen?
4. Can I forgive another easily?
5. Can I forgive myself?
6. Can I care for someone else more than I care for myself?

PRAYER FOR THE NEWLY MARRIED COUPLE

Let us ask God for his continued blessings upon this bridegroom
and his bride.

Holy Father, creator of the universe,
maker of man and woman in your own likeness,
source of blessing for married life,
we humbly pray to you for this woman
who today is united with her husband in this sacrament of marriage.

May your fullest blessing come upon her and her husband
so that they may together rejoice in your gift of married love
(and enrich your Church with their children).

Lord, may they both praise you when they are happy
and turn to you in their sorrows.
May they be glad that you help them in their work
and know that you are with them in their need.
May they pray to you in the community of the Church,
and be your witnesses in the world.
May they reach old age in the company of their friends,
and come at last to the kingdom of heaven.

We ask this through Christ our Lord.
Amen.

RITE OF MARRIAGE (N. 121)

APPENDIX A

Prayer

———

SCRIPTURE REFLECTION

He was praying in a certain place, and when he had finished, one of his disciples said to him, "Lord, teach us to pray just as John taught his disciples." He said to them, "When you pray, say:

Father, hallowed be your name,
    your kingdom come.
    Give us each day our daily bread
    and forgive us our sins
    for we ourselves forgive everyone in debt to us,
    and do not subject us to the final test."

LUKE 11:1-4

INTRODUCTION

Prayer integrates the Christian life before God. Prayer is relating one's self to God, listening to God, communicating with God, depending on God — and all these in combination. Prayer is raising one's heart and mind to God. Prayer can be personal and private. It can also be public and liturgical. Prayer uses words; it can also be soundless. Prayer can be spoken, sung, danced, or silent. Prayer may be loud. It may also be contemplative. Prayer expresses adoration of God, thanksgiving to God, petition from God, or contrition before God. In all cases, prayer reflects our situation in the presence of God. In the following section are some traditional examples of Christian prayer.

PRAYERS

THE EUCHARISTIC LITURGY, OR THE MASS

The most important form of Christian prayer and the central act of worship for the whole Church is the Eucharistic liturgy, or the Mass. The Mass is the ritual representation of the redemptive sacrifice of Christ, the living memorial of the life, death, and resurrection of the Lord. In the tradition of the Jewish Passover meal, when the Israelites mark their freedom from slavery in Egypt, Christians celebrate their passage from the slavery of sin to the freedom of life in Christ in the context of the ritual meal of the Eucharist. The one bread, the Body of Christ, and the one cup, the Blood of Christ, given and poured out for the many are shared in common table fellowship until he comes again. The following is an explanation of the usual parts of a Sunday liturgy.

The Order of Mass

The Mass begins with the *Introductory Rites*. These rites prepare the worshiping community for the Liturgy of the Word. The Entrance Song begins the Introductory Rites and gathers the assembly. The priest-celebrant then welcomes the assembly with the Greeting, in the name of the Blessed Trinity. Inviting the community to reflect on its sinfulness, the celebrant proclaims God's mercy in the Penitential Rite. The assembly then proclaims together the Gloria, the angels' prayer of praise to God. The Introductory Rites conclude with the Opening Prayer, which focuses the theme of the Mass.

The *Liturgy of the Word* proclaims Christ's presence in the living Word of Sacred Scripture. It begins with the Old Testament Reading, which ordinarily reveals an aspect of God's enduring love for the nation of Israel. The Responsorial Psalm follows and provides the people an opportunity for a reflective reply to the first reading. The lector then proclaims the New Testament Reading, which ordinarily reveals an aspect of God's enduring love for the early Christian community. Then the assembly sings an Alleluia or Gospel Acclamation in preparation for the proclamation of the Gospel. The priest or deacon then solemnly announces the Gospel, a selection from the testimonies of faith written by Matthew, Mark, Luke, or John. The priest or deacon explains the Word of God and relates it to the lives of the people in the Homily. The Liturgy of the Word concludes with the whole assembly's statement of its commonly held beliefs, the Profession of Faith.

The *Liturgy of the Eucharist* proclaims Christ's presence in the sacrament. It begins with the Preparation of the Gifts. This presentation of bread and wine by members of the assembly symbolizes the gift of our whole selves to God and our desire to receive him entirely. In the Prayer Over the Gifts, the celebrant then presents the gifts to God in the name of the assembly. In the Eucharistic Prayer the priest recalls God's saving action and speaks the words of Jesus at the Last Supper. In this living memorial Jesus is wholly present, and the gifts of bread and wine become the Body and Blood of Christ. The assembly acknowledges its participation in the sacrifice of Jesus through its proclamation of the "Amen" to conclude the Eucharistic Prayer.

The *Communion Rite* focuses on the worshiping community's incorporation into the Body of Christ. It begins with the Lord's Prayer, the words of Jesus that join the community to the Lord in prayer. Then the priest or deacon invites the people to share a Sign of Peace, which joins the community to the Lord in action. The Breaking of the Bread follows. Those who are properly disposed receive Holy Communion, an action that joins the individual and the community to the sacrificial sacrifice of Christ. After a brief period of reflection, the priest-celebrant leads the assembly in the Prayer After Communion, which gives thanks to God for the gift of Christ in the Eucharist.

The *Concluding Rite* brings the Mass to a fitting close. It begins with the Greeting followed immediately by the Blessing, which invokes the gracious presence of God in the lives of the community. The Dismissal invites the assembly to depart in peace and take up the mission of Christ in their daily lives. The Recessional Song gathers the voices of the worshiping community together as the ministers depart.

THE LITURGY OF THE HOURS

In addition to the Eucharist and the other sacraments, the Liturgy of the Hours is included in the official worship of the Church. Bishops, priests, and deacons are required to say the Liturgy of the Hours daily, either privately or in common, but it may be said by all the faithful. It is the daily prayer of the Church, which is rooted in the Eucharist and extends the Eucharistic themes of praise and thanksgiving throughout the day in a genuine harmony The Liturgy of the Hours draws heavily from the Scriptures for its structure and content, especially from the Psalms, which in itself is a handbook of prayer. Basically, the structure of the Liturgy of the Hours is as follows: Morning Prayer, Daytime Prayer, Evening Prayer, and Night Prayer. The Office of Readings may be said at any time during the day.

EXPOSITION AND BENEDICTION OF THE BLESSED SACRAMENT

Worship of the Eucharist outside of Mass is an important recognition of the presence of Christ that grows out of and leads back to the Mass. Exposition, or the public display of the Blessed Sacrament, makes it clear that Christ is available to us as food, healing, and consolation. The adoration of the Blessed Sacrament that takes place while the Eucharist is exposed can be accompanied by readings from Scripture, by prayers, and by songs that direct the people to the worship of Christ the Lord, who is actually present there. A homily is usually given to develop a better understanding of the Eucharist among the people. The Liturgy of the Hours may be recited during the exposition as well. Benediction, or the blessing of the people with the Eucharist, is usually accompanied by silence. The Divine Praises are often said after the blessing of the faithful. The Blessed Sacrament is then replaced in the tabernacle.

THE WAY OF THE CROSS

During the season of Lent, the Church is particularly aware of the redemptive sacrifice of Christ on the cross. Many Catholics gather to commemorate the suffering of Christ on the way to his death. The Stations of the Cross provide Catholics the opportunity to reflect on the different stages of Jesus' passion and death. Here are the traditional stations on the Way of the Cross:

1. Jesus Is Condemned to Death
2. Jesus Accepts His Cross
3. Jesus Falls the First Time
4. Jesus Meets His Mother
5. Simon Helps Jesus to Carry His Cross
6. Veronica Wipes the Face of Jesus
7. Jesus Falls the Second Time
8. Jesus Meets the Women of Jerusalem
9. Jesus Falls the Third Time
10. Jesus Is Stripped of His Clothes
11. Jesus Is Nailed to the Cross
12. Jesus Dies on the Cross
13. Jesus Is Taken Down From the Cross
14. Jesus Is Placed in the Tomb

THE SIGN OF THE CROSS

The Sign of the Cross is a simple but profound prayer that proclaims Christian belief in the Triune God and at the same time demonstrates faith in the saving action of Jesus. A cross is traced by the right hand, beginning from the forehead, moving to the breast, and then from the left shoulder to the right shoulder while saying, "In the name of the Father, and of the Son, and of the Holy Spirit. Amen."

Our Father (The Lord's Prayer)

Our Father, who art in heaven, hallowed be thy name; thy kingdom come; thy will be done on earth as it is in heaven. Give us this day our daily bread; and forgive us our trespasses as we forgive those who trespass against us; and lead us not into temptation, but deliver us from evil. Amen.

Hail Mary

Hail, Mary, full of grace, the Lord is with thee; blessed art thou among women, and blessed is the fruit of thy womb, Jesus.

Holy Mary, Mother of God, pray for us sinners, now and at the hour of our death. Amen.

Glory Be to the Father

Glory be to the Father, and to the Son, and to the Holy Spirit. As it was in the beginning, is now, and ever shall be, world without end. Amen.

Apostles' Creed

I believe in God, the Father almighty,
    creator of heaven and earth.

I believe in Jesus Christ, his only Son, our Lord.
    He was conceived by the power of the Holy Spirit
        and born of the Virgin Mary.
    He suffered under Pontius Pilate,
        was crucified, died, and was buried.
    He descended to the dead.
    On the third day he arose again.
    He ascended into heaven,

and is seated at the right hand of the Father.
He will come again to judge the living and the dead.

I believe in the Holy Spirit,
  the holy catholic Church,
  the communion of saints,
  the forgiveness of sins,
  the resurrection of the body,
  and the life everlasting. Amen.

MORNING PRAYER (CANTICLE OF ZECHARIAH; LUKE 1:68-79)

Blessed be the Lord, the God of Israel;
he has come to his people and set them free.

He has raised up for us a mighty savior,
born of the house of his servant David.

Through his holy prophets he promised of old
  that he would save us from our enemies,
  from the hands of all who hate us.

He promised to show mercy to our fathers
and to remember his holy covenant.

This was the oath he swore to our father Abraham:
to set us free from the hands of our enemies,
free to worship him without fear,
holy and righteous in his sight
  all the days of our life.
You, my child, shall be called the prophet of the Most High;
for you will go before the Lord to prepare his way,

to give his people knowledge of salvation
by the forgiveness of their sins.

In the tender compassion of our God
the dawn from on high shall break upon us,
to shine on those who dwell in darkness and the shadow of death,
and to guide our feet into the way of peace.

EVENING PRAYER (CANTICLE OF MARY, OR THE MAGNIFICAT; LUKE 1:46-55)
My soul proclaims the greatness of the Lord,
my spirit rejoices in God my Savior
for he has looked with favor on his lowly servant.

From this day all generations will call me blessed:
the Almighty has done great things for me,
and holy is his Name.

He has mercy on those who fear him
in every generation.

He has shown the strength of his arm,
he has scattered the proud in their conceit.

He has cast down the mighty from their thrones,
and has lifted up the lowly.

He has filled the hungry with good things,
and the rich he has sent away empty.

He has come to the help of his servant Israel
for he has remembered his promise of mercy,

the promise he made to our fathers,
to Abraham and his children for ever.

ACT OF CONTRITION

My God, I am sorry for all my sins with all my heart. In choosing to do wrong and failing to do good, I have sinned against you whom I should love above all things. I firmly intend, with your help, to do penance, to sin no more, and to avoid whatever leads me to sin. Our Savior, Jesus Christ, suffered and died for us. In his name, my God, have mercy. Amen.

Alternative prayer: Lord, Jesus Christ, Son of the living God, have mercy on me, a sinner.

ACT OF FAITH

O my God, I believe that you are one God in three divine persons: Father, Son, and Holy Spirit. I believe that your divine Son became man and died for our sins, and that he will come to judge the living and the dead. I believe these and all the truths the Catholic Church teaches, because you have revealed them, who can neither deceive nor be deceived. Amen.

ACT OF HOPE

O my God, relying on your almighty power and infinite mercy and promises, I hope to obtain pardon of my sins, the help of your grace, and life everlasting through the merits of Jesus Christ, my Lord and Redeemer. Amen.

ACT OF LOVE

O my God, I love you above all things with my whole heart and soul, because you are all good and worthy of all my love. I love my neighbor as myself for the love of you. I forgive all who have injured me and ask pardon of all whom I have injured. Amen.

THE ROSARY

The Rosary is a prayerful devotion to Mary, the Mother of God. The rosary that is held is a string of beads, each of which marks the recitation of a particular prayer. There are twenty groups of ten Hail Marys that form the central part of the Rosary. Each decade of the Rosary focuses on a mystery or event in the life of Jesus and Mary. The mysteries are clustered into four groups of five each to commemorate the joyful, sorrowful, glorious, and luminous events in the lives of Jesus and Mary. Here are the twenty mysteries of the Rosary:

The Joyful Mysteries
1. The Annunciation to Mary
2. The Visitation of Mary
3. The Nativity of Our Lord
4. The Presentation of Jesus in the Temple
5. The Finding of Jesus in the Temple

The Luminous Mysteries
1. The Baptism in the Jordan
2. The Wedding at Cana
3. The Proclamation of the Kingdom
4. The Transfiguration
5. The Institution of the Eucharist

The Sorrowful Mysteries
1. The Agony in the Garden
2. The Scourging at the Pillar
3. The Crowning With Thorns
4. The Carrying of the Cross
5. The Crucifixion

The Glorious Mysteries

1. The Resurrection of Jesus
2. The Ascension of Jesus
3. The Descent of the Holy Spirit Upon the Apostles
4. The Assumption of Mary
5. The Coronation of Mary as Queen of Heaven

The person begins to pray the Rosary by recalling which group of mysteries corresponds to the day on which the Rosary is being said. (The Joyful Mysteries are usually said on Monday and Saturday, the Luminous Mysteries on Thursday, the Sorrowful Mysteries on Tuesday and Friday, and the Glorious Mysteries on Wednesday and Sunday.) Then the person makes the Sign of the Cross. Next the Apostles' Creed is said while holding the crucifix attached to the rosary. One Our Father, three Hail Marys, and a Glory Be follow. Then the person reflects on the first mystery and says an Our Father, ten Hail Marys, and a Glory Be. This completes one decade of the Rosary. All other decades are said in the same way, with a different mystery reflected on during each. At the completion of five decades, the person may choose to conclude the Rosary by saying another Marian prayer, the *Memorare*.

MEMORARE

Remember, O most gracious Virgin Mary, that never was it known that anyone who fled to your protection, implored your help, or sought your intercession was left unaided. Inspired by this confidence, I fly unto you, O Virgin of virgins, my Mother! To you I come, before you I stand, sinful and sorrowful. O Mother of the Word Incarnate, despise not my petitions, but in your mercy, hear and answer me. Amen.

ANGELUS

Traditionally the *Angelus* is said at 6:00 a.m., 12:00 p.m., and 6:00 p.m.

Leader: The angel of the Lord declared unto Mary.

All: And she conceived of the Holy Spirit.

Hail Mary ...

Leader: Behold the handmaid of the Lord.

All: Be it done unto me according to your word.

Hail Mary ...

Leader: And the Word was made flesh.

All: And dwelt among us.

Hail Mary ...

Leader: Pray for us, O holy Mother of God.

All: That we may be made worthy of the promises of Christ.

Leader: Let us pray.

All: Pour forth, we beseech you, O Lord, your grace into our hearts, that we to whom the Incarnation of Christ, your Son, was made known by the message of an angel, may by his Passion and cross be brought to the glory of his Resurrection. Through the same Christ our Lord. Amen.

PRAYER BEFORE MEALS

Bless us, O Lord, and these your gifts, which we are about to receive from your bounty. Through Christ, our Lord. Amen.

PRAYER AFTER MEALS

We give you thanks, almighty God, for these and all your benefits, who lives and reigns forever and ever. Amen.

Other Catholic Practices

─────────

SEASONS OF THE CHURCH YEAR

The prayer of the Church, the central part of which is the celebration of the sacraments, is always set in the context of the liturgical seasons of the Church year. Whether personal, communal, or official, the prayer life of the Church unfolds the entire mystery of Christ through the various seasons of the liturgical year. A particular color is associated with each of the liturgical seasons. The liturgical seasons of the year are:

Advent: This season begins the Church year and comprises the four weeks prior to Christmas. The theme of this season is expectant hope for the coming of the Lord (purple).

Christmas: This season begins on Christmas Eve and extends until the feast of the Baptism of the Lord, usually in the second week of January. The theme of the season is joy rooted in the mystery of God becoming human in the person of Jesus (white).

Ordinary Time: This season extends from the feast of the Baptism of the Lord until Ash Wednesday, which is usually in late February or early March. The theme of Ordinary Time is the central mystery of our redemption in Christ (green).

Lent: This season begins on Ash Wednesday and lasts until Holy Thursday, the Thursday before Easter. The theme of this season is penitential preparation for the commemoration of the Passion, Death, and Resurrection of the Lord (purple).

The Triduum: The most important days of the Church year are called the Triduum, or "three days": Holy Thursday, Good Friday, and Easter. Each day has a distinctive theme in connection with the Paschal mystery of Jesus (white, red, white, respectively).

Easter: This season extends from Easter Sunday until Pentecost, usually in late May or early June. The theme is our freedom from sin and death to a life of grace in Christ (white).

Ordinary Time: This season extends from Pentecost Sunday through the feast of Christ the King and the last week in Ordinary Time, which is usually in late November. The theme celebrated by the Church during Ordinary Time is our redemption in Christ. (Green)

HOLY DAYS OF OBLIGATION

In addition to all of the Sundays of the year, several days are set aside by the United States Conference of Catholic Bishops to commemorate some of the major events in the life of Jesus, Mary, and the saints. Catholics are obliged to celebrate the Eucharistic liturgy on these days. While there are some variations in the celebration of the holy days of obligation according to the particular region of the country, in the United States they are:

December 8: Solemnity of the Immaculate Conception of the Blessed Virgin Mary

December 25: Solemnity of the Nativity of the Lord

January 1: Solemnity of the Blessed Virgin Mary, Mother of God

Thursday of the Sixth Week of Easter: Solemnity of the Ascension of the Lord

August 15: Solemnity of the Assumption of the Blessed Virgin Mary

November 1: Solemnity of All Saints

The obligation to attend Mass is set aside in the United States whenever Mary, Mother of God (January 1), the Assumption (August 15), or All Saints (November 1) falls on a Saturday or Monday.

THEOLOGICAL VIRTUES

The theological virtues are faith, hope, and charity. *Faith* is the good habit of being firmly convinced that God has revealed himself in Christ, the way to salvation. *Hope* is the good habit of being firmly convinced that the Kingdom of God will come. *Charity* is the good habit of being filled with God's love and being transformed by it.

THE BEATITUDES

Blessed are the poor in spirit; the reign of God is theirs (dependence on God, the virtue of religion, piety).

Blessed are the sorrowing; they shall be consoled (hope, contrition, compassion).

Blessed are the lowly; they shall inherit the land (reliance on God, trust, humility, hope).

Blessed are they who hunger and thirst for holiness; they shall have their fill (submission to God's will, justice, righteousness).

Blessed are they who show mercy; mercy shall be theirs (forgiveness, patience, understanding, compassion).

Blessed are the single-hearted; they shall see God (right judgment, prudence, obedience).

Blessed are the peacemakers; they shall be called sons of God (reconciliation, justice).

Blessed are those persecuted for holiness' sake; the reign of God is theirs (piety, resignation, justice, patience).

THE SPIRITUAL AND CORPORAL WORKS OF MERCY

Human mercy can be extended to another because God has first extended his mercy to us. Mercy extended to another expresses our solidarity with the other and our common need for redemption in Christ. The Spiritual and Corporal Works of Mercy have been practiced by Christians to demonstrate their obligations to others in need, but they are not to be seen as minimal requirements of the law. Rather, they extend from the love of God abiding in the Christian heart and are concrete acts of genuine service. Some examples are:

The Spiritual Works of Mercy
To admonish the sinner
To instruct the ignorant
To counsel the doubtful
To comfort the sorrowful
To bear wrongs patiently
To forgive all injuries
To pray for the living and the dead

The Corporal Works of Mercy
To feed the hungry
To give drink to the thirsty
To clothe the naked
To visit those in prison
To shelter the homeless
To visit the sick
To bury the dead

THE PRECEPTS OF THE CHURCH

The Church has the responsibility of providing for its own good order and, therefore, has the authority to list certain duties for its members. Once again, performance of these duties does not merit the person salvation, because salvation is not earned by the person but freely offered by Christ to the person. Nevertheless, these precepts of the Church are important reminders of how to live the Christian life. In the United States, they are:

1. To celebrate the Eucharist on Sundays and holy days of obligation and to avoid unnecessary and inappropriate work on Sunday.
2. To celebrate the sacraments frequently, confessing mortal sins at least once a year, and receiving Holy Communion during the Easter season.
3. To study Catholic teaching in preparation for Confirmation and to be confirmed.
4. To observe the marriage laws of the Church.
5. To contribute to the support of the Church.
6. To do penance at the appropriate times.
7. To join in the missionary spirit and apostolate of the Church.

REGULATIONS FOR FAST AND ABSTINENCE

Personal acts of penance are important experiences in the continual conversion of the Christian to the life of grace. They insert us into the suffering of Jesus, who, in turn, gives meaning to our penitential acts. Acts of self-denial, personal charity, and prayer deprive the self and surrender the self for the sake of another. They display a humble and contrite heart, one that understands that doing good for a person in need exacts a personal price that is gladly paid out of love for God. Caring for those in need, fasting from food for periods of time, and abstaining from meat on designated days are all meaningful only insofar as they are related to a wider understanding of penance and conversion in the Christian life.

To *fast* means to deprive oneself of a certain amount of food for a certain length of time. To *abstain* means to deprive oneself of meat. Ash Wednesday and Good Friday are days on which Catholics are to eat only one full meal (fast) and eat no meat at all (abstain). The Fridays of Lent are days on which no meat is to be eaten (abstinence).

Eating only one full meal, and two smaller meals (with both smaller meals not equaling the full meal), with no eating between meals (fasting) applies to healthy people between the ages of 18 and 59. Eating no meat (abstaining) applies to all those over 14. Those who have an appropriate reason for modifying the law are not obliged to fast.

Index

Our Sunday Visitor …
Your Source for Discovering
the Riches of the Catholic Faith

Our Sunday Visitor has an extensive line of materials for young children, teens, and adults. Our books, Bibles, pamphlets, CD-ROMs, audios, and videos are available in bookstores worldwide.

To receive a FREE full-line catalog or for more information, call **Our Sunday Visitor** at **1-800-348-2440, ext. 3**. Or write **Our Sunday Visitor** / 200 Noll Plaza / Huntington, IN 46750.

Please send me ___ A catalog
Please send me materials on:
___ Apologetics and catechetics
___ Prayer books
___ The family
___ Reference works
___ Heritage and the saints
___ The parish

Name _____
Address _____ Apt._____
City _____ State _____ Zip_____
Telephone (   ) _____
                                                    A59BBBBP

Please send a friend ___ A catalog
Please send a friend materials on:
___ Apologetics and catechetics
___ Prayer books
___ The family
___ Reference works
___ Heritage and the saints
___ The parish

Name _____
Address _____ Apt._____
City _____ State _____ Zip_____
Telephone (   ) _____
                                                    A59BBBBP

OurSundayVisitor

200 Noll Plaza, Huntington, IN 46750
Toll free: **1-800-348-2440**
Website: www.osv.com